1/90

# Hugh Newell Jacobsen, Architect

Designed and edited by Massimo Vignelli
Photographs by Robert Lautman
Introduction by Vincent Scully, Hon. AIA

Text edited by Kevin W. Green

The American Institute of Architects Press
Washington, D.C.

© 1988 by the American Institute of Architects.
All rights reserved. Published 1988. Printed in
Hong Kong by Everbest Printing Co., Ltd.

91   90   89   88   7   6   5   4   3   2   1

*Library of Congress Cataloging in Publication Data*
Jacobsen, Hugh Newell.
Hugh Newell Jacobsen, architect/Hugh Newell
Jacobsen; Robert Lautman, photographer;
introduction by Vincent Scully; foreword by
Massimo Vignelli.
p. cm.
ISBN 0-913962-97-X: $50.00. ISBN 0-913962-95-3
(pbk.): $35.00.
1. Jacobsen, Hugh Newell—Catalogs. 2. Architecture,
Modern—20th century—United States—Catalogs.
I. Lautman, Robert C.
II. Title.
NA737.J3A4   1988
720′.92′4—dc19
88–11468

Production by Meadows & Wiser
Type in Devinne by Carver Photocomposition, Inc.

Dust jacket and cover: St. Peter's Church, Olney,
Maryland

# Contents

The house, more than any other form of building, seems to be the essence of Hugh Newell Jacobsen's search for architecture. Although through his work he has proven to be a masterful hand on any kind of building, his achievement of the notion of the house as the place for staging life is rarely paralleled by other architects.

Jacobsen achieves his expression through a lifelong refinement of the plan, articulating it to set, propose, and develop situations. A master of placing the houses in their environmental, cultural, and historic contexts, Jacobsen has managed to define, refine, and articulate his architectural language to express at the same time diversity and identity. A Jacobsen house is a Jacobsen house, recognizable not by mere tangible icons, but by the essence of it, the articulation of the intangibles.

Although many of the best contemporary architects seem to be interested in expressing theoretical positions in their architecture, very few have been able to develop better than Jacobsen the notion of the house as a building type. From the first to the last project, Jacobsen's plans are designed not as abstractions but as sequences, implying a viewer, a person approaching the house, entering it, and proceeding through it. Vistas are carefully planned, functions are transformed into spaces, materials are selected to express the essence of that particular house. Even if his projects span from International Style to American vernacular or neo-Gothic to Greek Revivalism, Jacobsen should not be considered an eclectic since his projects are unmistakably Jacobsen in essence and form.

The remodeling of a Victorian House in Washington sets the pace for all his urban projects, like the Trentman House (with the beautiful stairwell lit by the skylight) or Jacobsen's own house in Washington. These projects are distinguished by a particular respect for an urban quality of architecture, which is found as well in his buildings for Georgetown University. Along with Jacobsen's urban projects, the restorations of important historic buildings such as the Renwick Gallery, the Smithsonian Museum in Washington, and the Hotel Talleyrand on Place de la Concorde in Paris once again attest to his sensitivity and respect for the original buildings, elegantly interpreted and re-presented to us. The Hotel Talleyrand in particular stands as one of the most beautiful restorations of a building that had fallen into the hands of insensitive bureaucrats. In its new definition, the Hotel Talleyrand stands indeed as a new landmark.

In the Brick Pavilioned House we begin to see the notion of pavilions on a podium, which becomes a recurrent approach throughout his work. The podium, the acropolis of the house, is a classical reference, conferring status to the building and its owners. The Putterman House, the House in Kentucky, the Challinor House, the Karpidas House, and several more all stand assertively on podiums.

In the Blumenthal House, Jacobsen arrives at the formulation of his own language, which he had been refining from the beginning. In this house, we find all the elements of Jacobsen's architecture: the articulation of the roofs, the recessed entrance, the double chimney stack, the interior spaces, the ceilings high to the roof, the flush gutters, the white skin.

The House in the Virgin Islands epitomizes the notion of the resort house, intended as a spectacular sequence of exterior-interior spaces where light and shadows play a joyous game. The pool area expresses Jacobsen's ability to give grand scale to these open spaces, as we can see as well in the pool area of the House in Kentucky.

The compound of the Dixon houses, black against the white snow, represents the first dramatic perception of the house as a village. This exciting notion will become a benchmark of Jacobsen's work. The Bryan House, the Mendoza House, and the Jacobs, Carson, and Waddell Houses are all refinements of this wonderful concept, rooted in the heritage of the American house.

The Buckwalter House represents the wit of a genius. The house, like a telescope, expands from a little Colonial cabin into a major house. The cross section is covered only by reflective glass that, as in Magritte, mirrors the sky and dematerializes the house. From the inside, the house opens to the landscape one step at a time toward a grand finale of wall-to-wall views. In his eighteenth-century wit and sense of elegance, Jacobsen loves to risk everything to the breaking point, to survive as the winner.

On top of a rolling field in Kentucky, with horses, white fences, and beautiful trees on a white acropolis rests a house, Greek Revival in spirit, pure Jacobsen in its form. This superb white house with white brick columns is as Jeffersonian as Monticello, poised in the landscape, serene, and dignified.

The Challinor House, a small wooden house on a wooden podium, is a delightful example of neoclassicism, scaled down to our times. Neoclassicism, again, is evident in the House on the Eastern Shore, with carefully planned views of perspectives and waters. And this, again, is Jacobsen at his best— placing the building in the land and changing the land to offer its best.

The Zamoiski House relates to its surroundings in a stimulating way, penetrating the bay with a long pier from the narrow side of the house, while the long side (a sequence of small buildings) is oriented toward lands and ponds. The Welles House, too, is a masterpiece in siting. The house is set near an abandoned bridge over a river; the house's many vistas of the bridge evoke old Roman ruins.

Jacobsen's passion for context is not limited to environmental situations, but goes beyond to involve historic or cultural references. In the Karpidas House, as in several other projects in Greece, Jacobsen evokes acropolis, colonnades, patios, and materials from the Greek heritage. But again the building is quintessentially Jacobsen.

The Rosenak House in New Mexico and the Kahn House in Ohio are delightful investigations into the nature of the Victorian house. While the first is a colorful interpretation of the false-front architecture of a frontier town, the second is a virtuosic exercise in neo-Gothic vernacular. Both houses represent a desire to probe forbidden lands of our culture. Both houses also represent a fascinating episode in Jacobsen's work.

The Bryan House is set on a hill near an old stone church and from this it retrieves its inspiration. The house becomes part of a language previously established by the old buildings nearby, and extends it further into our times. The Bryan House has a beautifully articulated plan that embraces the surrounding landscape, while the inner court, as in an old castle, becomes its powerful hub.

The house in the Dominican Republic epitomizes Jacobsen's sense of contextualism and his ability to develop the theme of resort house. Few other houses in the Caribbean, if any, look so Caribbean and so pleasant. The local vernacular has been borrowed, transformed, and wittily interpreted to create an extremely pleasant place.

The new projects at the end of the book represent the direction in which Jacobsen is moving now. They reflect the attitude of continuous refinement that we find throughout his work. Marvelously articulated plans, witty contextualism, and above all, a tremendous love and respect for architecture.

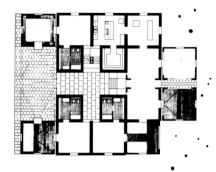

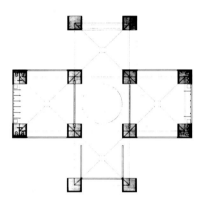

Louis I. Kahn's Trenton Bath House (top) and Fleisher House (bottom). Courtesy Louis I. Kahn Collection, University of Pennsylvania, and Pennsylvania Historical and Museum Commission.

Hugh Newell Jacobsen is a highly successful architect and, it is fair to say, a very fashionable one. His impressive array of well-tailored houses reflects the play of a fastidious mind upon the architectural events and the work of the most influential architects of the past 30 years. At the same time, he is a highly civilized, entirely professional architect with a serious, sincere, and cultivated interest in history and preservation. *A Guide to the Architecture of Washington, D.C.*, which he edited, set a standard for excellence in that field and has surely played a part in the preservation of some worthy buildings which might otherwise have sunk unseen under the advance of Development during the past two decades.

Something of the linear reductionism that defines all of Jacobsen's projects directly recalls the design of Philip Johnson of whatever epoch, and Jacobsen worked for Johnson immediately after graduating from architecture school in 1955. What might be called the "tone" of Jacobsen's work is thus Johnsonian throughout, alike in his International Style projects and his abstracted vernacular essays of recent years. More fundamental, though, in Jacobsen's shaping of architectural form is the influence of Louis I. Kahn, who was his teacher at Yale. The strict, rather stiff geometry of plan that pervades Jacobsen's work from first to last is thus invariably organized into discrete spatial units like those of Kahn, whose Fleisher House project in 1959 is recalled in almost every one of Jacobsen's designs. Jacobsen is by no means alone in this. A whole set of architects has based its domestic planning on that of the Fleisher House for almost a generation now, while another set, led by Venturi, has taken its point of departure in plan from Kahn's Goldenberg House project of exactly the same year. Two more different types of planning can hardly be imagined: the Goldenberg House pulls out from the center, flexible and asymmetrical, tending toward volumetric unity, while the Fleisher House is rigidly cubical, symmetrical, and strictly compartmented, wholly articulating part from part.

That kind of planning clearly responds to Jacobsen's instinct for precision, clarity, and elegant formality, and all his buildings and projects share those qualities. Beyond that, however, they follow an interesting course of development in terms of influence. First, in the Naftalin and Thoron Houses, it is Kahn of the Trenton Bath House, exactly as it was for Charles Moore in the same years and, perhaps in part, for Venturi in his Beach House project of 1959. Next it is Johnson in the Gainer House, Brick-Pavilioned House, and Millett House; then, in all likelihood, Rudolph, in Bolton Square, the Harvey House, Tidesfall, the House in the Virgin Islands, and the Housing Project for Pennsylvania Avenue—all employing the rather unhappy device of poke-through side walls, lifted up higher than the roof. There are others in that vein, and a few in the semi-European, broken shed-roofed, pseudo-vernacular, Corbusier-derived, with which Stirling and others were experimenting in the early sixties. The latter has remained in Jacobsen's repertory ever since. Then the Trenton Bath House returns in the Baker House (they are all called "Residences" in Jacobsen's publications) and Half Moon Bay.

In the eighties the range of interest becomes wider and in some instances surprising. We have the feeling that Jacobsen is entering into his own decade. There are the expected influences from Venturi and, especially, Rossi. The renderings become haunting, perhaps a little like some of those employed by Johnson but with a strong sense of Rossi and Leon Krier. Pennsylvania farmhouses are elongated and eviscerated; a house in New Mexico becomes a false-fronted street in the desert, painted with its own pale shadows under the New Mexican sun. Greek Revival megara take shape in Connecticut, and Stanley Tigerman's black barn proliferates in Minnesota. Dutch-gabled houses and Trenton Bath Houses are projected for Holland, and the fantastic vision of a "Homeric" palace—"where Agamemnon should have lived," says Jacobsen—with outsize columns (Rob Krier, Venturi, Johnson, Wright), some of them chromed, is set down in Greece. It is the architecture of the affluent decade, clearly jet-setted, spreading everywhere.

Preservation and contextualism come into play. A powerfully antiseptic Victorian Gothic mass is constructed at Gettysburg, and a handsome Gothick Folly in Ohio. Good, straight, student housing in brick with a fine cornice is built for Georgetown, and the Hotel Talleyrand is renovated for the State Department in Paris. Photographed in it, Jacobsen looks more like a distinguished diplomat than any of the poor fellows who actually do the job.

Given the critical climate of the eighties, there is nothing surprising in any of this work. Like the earlier buildings, it is all defined and distinguished by Jacobsen's thin, taut line and his reticent economy of detail. It is everywhere abstracted from its sources. Perhaps for that reason, the major surprise in Jacobsen's recent work should not come as a surprise at all. That is the revival in it of a lush, if puristic, International Style mode of design. His project for Lexington, Kentucky, is in that vein, an extensive columned pavilion recalling the work of Johnson, Bunschaft, and Kevin Roche. Another is the house at McLean, Virginia, primarily a lucid glass box with a book-encased service core suggesting Philip Johnson's at New Canaan. There are other examples as well, some masquerading, like a house in the Maryland Tidewater, under a series of frontal gables, but all International Style pavilions nonetheless—in this case employing bay-scaled shutters like those used by Rudolph in the early fifties.

In general, it seems that this is the way of design that is most truly natural to Jacobsen. It is what his instincts lead him to do, and its virtues shape all of his other works, whatever their incidental disguise of the moment may be. It is the kind of architecture, after all, that Jacobsen was trained to do, the kind that was normal for his generation. And Jacobsen is supremely good at it, clearly loving its cleanness, coolness, and excellent manners. If his more vernacular projects of the decade look a little thin, overrefined, and remote, and if they often seem to rarefy the vernacular out of all body, such can hardly be otherwise. His heart can be only partially in them. He is compelled to abstract them, reduce them, clean them up. In this he is a limpid reflection of his time and his training. He is a fashionable architect of the later twentieth century in the United States, and a good one.

# Thoron House

*Suburban Maryland*

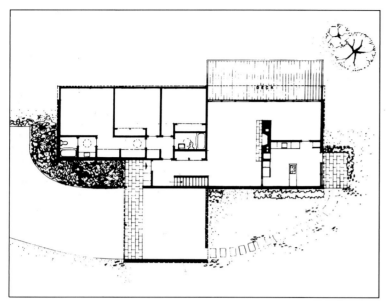

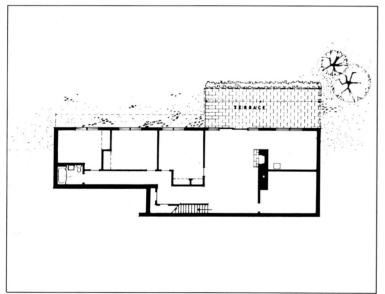

The hillside site of this house falls rapidly away at a 45-degree slope from its street frontage, and the design of the house responds directly to the topography. Because the house is first perceived from above, at street level, the roof serves as a primary facade. Painted brick expresses the bearing walls, and round skylights offer visual relief from the roof-as-facade.

Overlooking a suburban woodland park, the house was designed so that every room would enjoy the view through the treetops. Both levels have identical floor plans, with a children's zone on the lower level and the parents' and formal living areas on the entry floor.

The living room and dining room are divided by a large, brick chimney mass that is expressed on all levels. Both rooms open onto a deck whose surround of trees reflects seasonal colors throughout the house. Industrial-hopper sashes and steel sliding-glass doors were installed to complete the sought-after order of the brick-and-glass houses that were appearing in the architectural journals of the day.

# A Victorian House Remodeled

*Georgetown, Washington, D.C.*

Originally built a century ago as a speculative row house in Georgetown, this "Tuscan villa" was produced in the Italianate style very much in vogue at the time. Faced with pressed brick, the house was detailed with crenellations, dentils, and a pedimented, two-story bay, with a single entry to the left. After the adjacent vacant lot was acquired at a later date, a new entrance was created on the long, eastern facade, allowing an enchanting approach to the door through a sunny city garden. By the middle of this century, however, the Italianate design had been "Georgianized" with multipaned windows, painted brick, and other incursions that left the house visually, as well as actually, uncomfortable.

Lowering the windows of the existing house to the floor was a deliberate attempt to make the house look like a custom-designed Italianate house, setting it off not only from its immediate neighbors but from the row after row of nearly identical houses that continued to be built throughout Washington. The addition repeats the now-altered facade of the pedimented bay and allows enough room for a formal entry. The new "H" plan permits a glass-roofed foyer that shares the side facades of both the original house and the new addition. While the street facade carries on the scale, rhythm, and proportion of the historic Georgetown street, the rear facades abstract this verticality and allow views of the terraced, Lester Collins-designed garden, with its large, lily-filled pool and glorious weeping cherry tree.

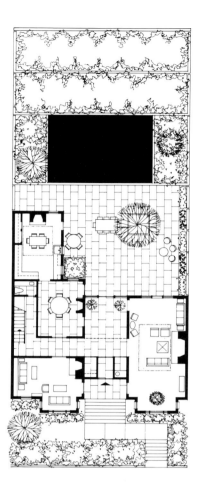

Opposite. The garden facade.

Above. The garden is enjoyed
from the "bridge" connecting
the new master bedroom to the
original house.

# Shorb House

*Bethesda, Maryland*

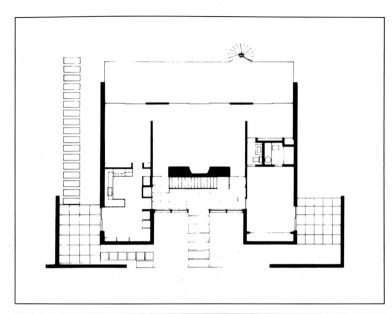

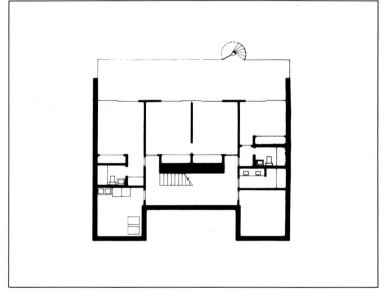

This house was designed for a wooded site sloping toward the Potomac River some distance away. The surrounding land is occupied by formidable oak trees that establish a scale all their own and admit a quality of light that sparkles against the tough blackness of the trunks.

The deliberate symmetry of the house asserts its presence in this stand of oaks. Man is nature, and his order is a part of nature; order, proportion, scale, and straight lines are the elements that proclaim the presence of man upon the land, and this house is no exception. Its brick exterior, however, is unpainted, presenting a nearly unique skin that is not unlike the rind of a Camembert.

The proscenium entry announces the chimney mass as the center—hearth and home—and promises not only something on the other side of this mass but something below as well, evidenced by the stairs down to a lower level. The exterior brick walls, while defining the enclosure as it turns its respective corners, become two stories in height as the site falls away to the rear. Here the masonry ends and the entire rear facade is glazed from floor to ceiling. The upper-level rooms are linked by sliding-glass doors to a broad deck that runs the entire length of the house. A spiral exterior stair joins the upper deck to a stone terrace below.

The tyranny of symmetry can be diverting, and the results can range from forced to boring to beautifully simple. In the end, the plan must work. In most good buildings, it does.

# Beech House

*West Tisbury, Massachusetts*

This house is on the island of Martha's Vineyard, where the landscape is dominated by trees and the marine light, with its blue shadow. A four-foot overhang, requested by the owner, provides protection from surprise squalls and glare. The exterior is clad in red Tidewater cypress, which was also used for the interior trim and living room ceiling. The roof is a prudent cement tile resembling cedar shake. The cypress has now weathered to silver and gray in harmony with the factory-weathered roof. The interior floors are cork throughout. The topknots on the roof conceal skylights and vent pipes. The exterior gutters are copper and have not yet oxidized to the longed-for green.

In a deliberate attempt to reduce the scale of the house, the massing of the building reflects the elements of the plan—living/dining, kitchen, and sleeping areas. The living room reaches for light at its center through a large coffer, vertically lined with inch-square cypress strips, placed one inch apart. Each of the four bedrooms has two exposures. The interior spaces are served by pairs of single-light French doors made of cypress. The central pavilion is mostly floor-to-ceiling fixed glass, announcing the entry on one side and, on the other, opening the dining room to the full drama of the light and the view to Cutty Hunk Island on the near horizon.

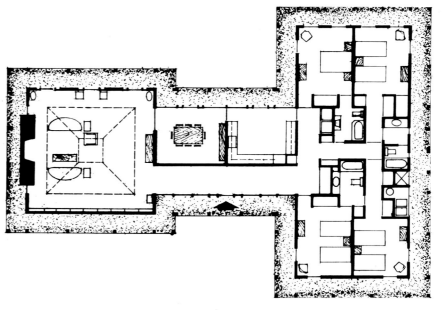

Top. The exterior of the house with the living room pavilion on the right.
Bottom. Looking across the terrace lawn toward the living room pavilion.

Opposite. From the living room, the entry is on the right and the dining room is on the left.

# Cafritz House

*Georgetown, Washington, D.C.*

This late-19th-century Italianate row house in historic Georgetown occupies the middle of its row and is a tidy 18 feet wide. The clients were a young family with two energetic boys. The design challenge was to meet their program while recapturing the original architectural grace of this often-altered residence.

Changing the windows and the front door achieved a verticality that distinguishes the house from its neighbors without being rude. The brick had been painted pink; that was changed to a deep, warm gray trimmed with black. The result is neither Victorian nor modern, but it is certainly (and intentionally) polite. If nothing else, the original row house had good manners.

The interior was radically changed to meet the active program set out by the clients. The addition of a 10-foot extension on all levels made it possible to include a new spiral stair serving all four floors, which freed the plan considerably. Four large bedrooms were included, as was an outdoor terrace off the fourth floor. The living room overlooks, and the dining room opens onto, a stone-paved urban garden visually terminated by a fountain. The entire lower level is surfaced with the same stone that extends to the rear of the garden. An exterior spiral stair joins the living room to the terrace below.

The usual custom in the execution of speculative houses is to concentrate the architectural order on the street facade and to let the rear fend for itself. Here an effort was made to relate the garden facade to the interior spaces and the fenestration of the street facade; no building should possess an apologetic rear.

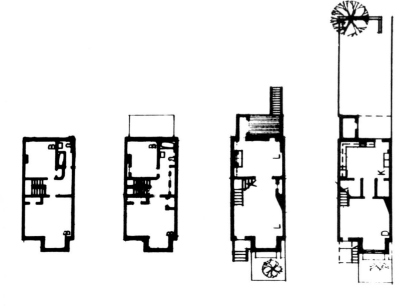

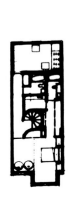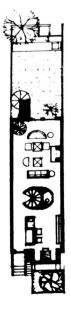

Upper-level living space with
fireplace and the dining room.

The spiral stair.

# A Brick-Pavilioned House

*Washington, D.C.*

Rock Creek Park is a seldom-sung wonder that
stretches through Washington from the Potomac River
to the northern Maryland suburbs and beyond. A wild,
green swatch of some 1,800 acres of forest and running
stream, it is but one of a series of parklands that define
neighborhoods and boundaries throughout the city.

From the beginning, this house adjoining the park was
conceived as a series of connected brick pavilions
resting on a podium, an island of calm on a hilly site.

Bay windows were used to extend the interior spaces,
defined by the brick walls of the house, and to bring
reflected natural light into the interior spaces, giving
them a quality of illumination like the light after a
snowfall.

Because of the terrain, the massing of the house was
accompanied by a change in level that permitted
"public" areas to be separate from private family areas.
Thus, the formal areas—living room, library, and
dining room—enjoy a 12-foot ceiling height, taking
advantage of the raised ceiling within the mansard,
while the bedrooms and other informal spaces are held
to eight feet in height.

The garden is a series of paved and green levels
designed to complement and reinforce the podium-
and-pavilion scheme. Lester Collins, FASLA, worked
closely with the architecture in his design of the
gardens.

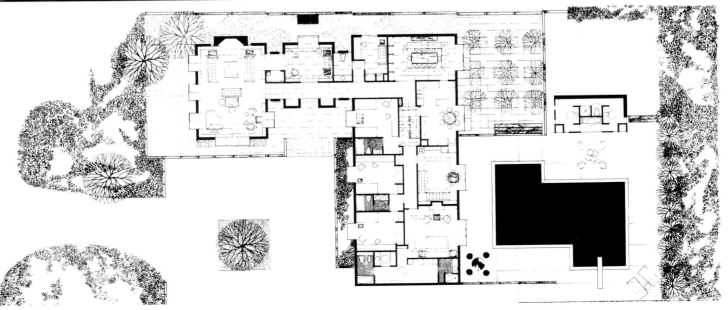

The front entry.

Top. The living room pavilion, park facade.

Bottom. The living room, park elevation.

# Millett House

*Bristol, Rhode Island*

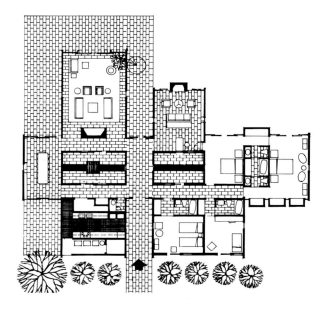

At first, the site of the Millett House was simply a knoll defined by a very old stone wall and a few elm trees stunted by seasons of bitter winds. Between the knoll and the road lay a restless meadow of tall grass and Queen Anne's lace. On the other side of the knoll, 300 yards of high, waving grass reached toward the broad expanse of Bristol Bay.

The program for a large house on this site was deliberately broken into seven interlocking pavilions to reduce its mass, to give form to the house, and, it is hoped, to retain the integrity of the knoll. The interior spaces of the pavilions rise to a height of 12 feet above the center of each pavilion's respective purpose—i.e., above the conversation area in the living room, above the dining room table, above the work area in the kitchen, above the desk in the library, above the beds. Eight-foot ceilings were relegated to circulation and support spaces.

The terraces and interiors are surfaced with natural-cleft stone. The two interior courts contain fountained pools designed to align with the slit windows and reinforce their common axis. The interior spaces are devoid of any kind of trim. The house is clad in tongue-and-groove red Tidewater cypress that has been left untreated to cure to a natural silver in the salt air. The program called for a maintenance-free house; to that end, the only surfaces requiring paint are the exterior downlights and the flat-black standing-seam roof. All openings are floor-to-ceiling fixed glass or black, anodized sliding-glass doors. Concealed gutters direct the flow of rainwater to the chain leaders that serve as downspouts.

Top. The living room and view
of Mt. Hope Bridge, beyond.

Bottom. The library and its
fireplace.

# Bolton Square

*Baltimore, Maryland*

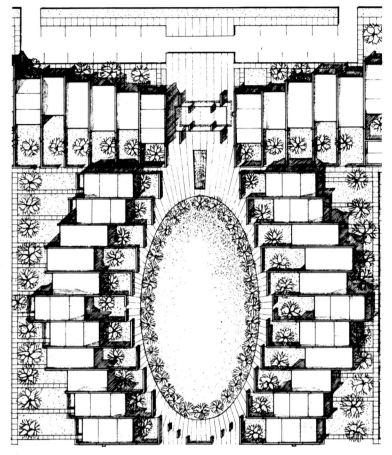

In an effort to prevent further blight in a downtown residential neighborhood, the Baltimore Urban Renewal Authority held a design competition for two blocks that had recently been cleared of badly deteriorated tenements. The blocks border on Bolton Hill, a proud and historically important section of the city with a recognizable heritage of 19th-century domestic architecture.

This competition-winning design consisted of 37 brick, single-family row houses based on four different plans, each with a front yard and a private, brick-walled garden facing a common enclosed park. Fenced off from the rest of the city, the new park is the exclusive domain of Bolton Square residents; it occupies the portion of the site that could not be built upon because of the underground utilities.

The burgundy brick and dark gray mortar with black window trim (deliberately borrowed from the successful architectural vocabulary nearby) allowed Bolton Square to fit comfortably into its older neighborhood. The use of brick was the key to catching the vertical rhythms existing along the street while maintaining the vitality of the area's domestic scale.

Top. A view of Bolton Square
from across the street.
Bottom. A group of row houses
with aligned facades.

Opposite. Private-walled
gardens.

Opposite. A two-story living room viewed from its walled garden.

Top. The dining room in one of the houses.
Center. The living room in the same house.
Bottom. Floor plans of one unit.

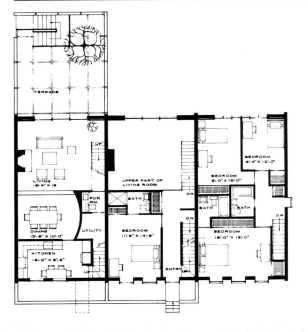

# Trentman House

*Georgetown, Washington, D.C.*

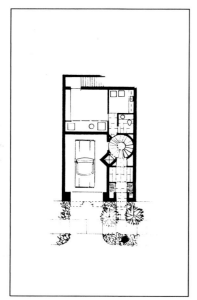
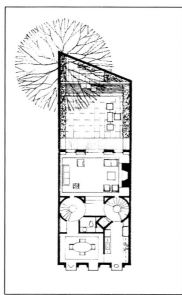

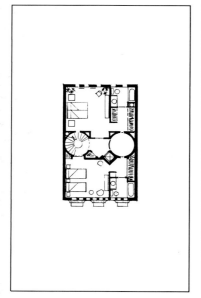
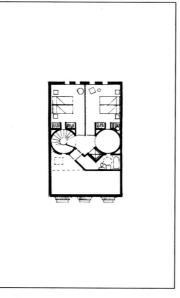

The federal Fine Arts Commission oversees the Georgetown historic district of Washington, D.C. The Trentman House replaced a late-19th-century, two-story, wood-frame house there, and it was closely monitored by both the commission and the community as the first piece of "deliberate modern architecture" to be erected since the enactment of Georgetown's historic designation by Congress.

Houses in this area of Georgetown range from early-19th-century workers' housing to early-Truman and late-Eisenhower colonial revivals. The strongest unifying elements here—as in other historic districts such as Charleston, Nantucket, and Savannah—are the scale of the houses and the transferral of this scale through the horizontal lines that are formed by cornices, window heads, sills, and lintels. These lines, when projected from neighboring houses across the space to be in-filled, established the dominant horizontal lines of the new house and helped form a polite compatibility. The vertical lines were developed as expressions of the interior spaces.

Since most of the natural light permitted in a row house must enter through the street and garden facades, the interiors tend to be dark. The center spaces of the Trentman House are served by two 10-foot-wide, 42-foot-tall cylinders that contain winding stairs; topped by clear skylights of equal diameter, these cylinders sparkle the interiors with sunlight. Because of the grade change of the site, the second-floor living room opens onto a rear garden; the dining room and kitchen face the tennis courts and the park across the street. The garden was designed with Lester Collins, FASLA.

Below. The garden facade.          Opposite. The front entry foyer,
                                   with stair beyond.

Top. The skylight above the stair. Opposite. The base of the
Bottom. A section of the house. winding stair.

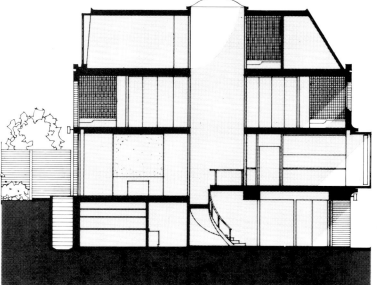

# Tidesfall

*Columbia, Maryland*

This subdivided site, with road and utilities already
in place, bordered a small lake in the new town of
Columbia. The zoning allowed a zero lot line, which
means that no setback from the property line to the
face of the building was required. Although portions of
the site faced a tree-lined gorge dotted with detached
houses, the longest stretch abutted the edge of the
new lake.

The row houses address the street with a high,
continuous wall that is penetrated by well-defined
garden gates beside flush garage doors. Once through
a house's gate, one is meant to traverse a sun-filled
forecourt with trees shading the route to the entry
door. In several of the five different models, there are
interior level changes that allow views of the woods or
the lake through large glazed openings in most of the
rooms. Tall masonry and stucco wing walls define the
wide wood decks that extend across the entire nonstreet
facade; the wing walls serve as sound and privacy
screens and offer protection from the wind as well.

The mixing and reversing of the floor plans have
provided an interesting variety of spaces, in part
because of the change in the quality of light from the
woods to the lake. The interior spaces themselves are
surprisingly large and work well for the families living
in them.

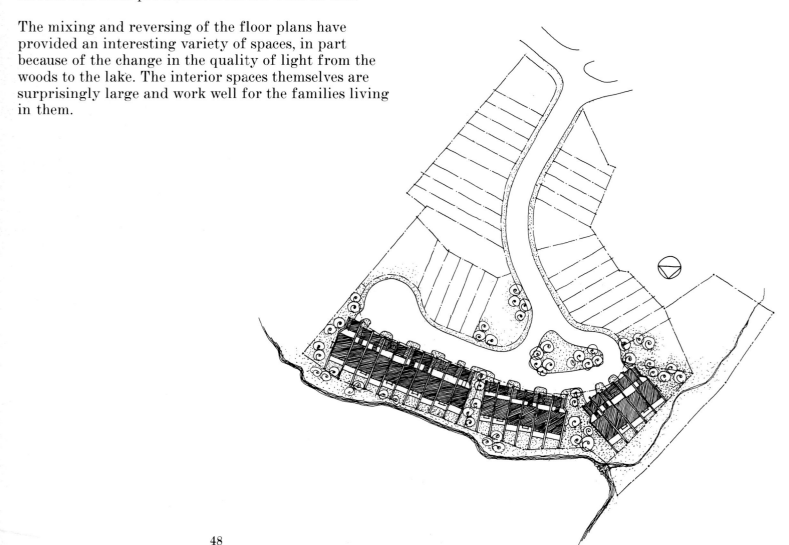

Top. Row houses that address the lake.
Center. Row houses on a court.
Bottom. Floor plans.

Opposite. Upper- and lower-level garden facade at night.

# Blumenthal House

*Eastern Shore, Maryland*

Fifty years ago, the owner's father scattered cedar seedlings on the future site of this house, which faces the mouth of a wide river with the Chesapeake Bay close at hand. Today, the tall cedar grove protects the land from the sometimes severe winter storms that come in off the water.

The shoreline here is but a turning in from the broad reaches of the bay. Someone once said, "The Tidewater is the one place on earth where the sea meets the land gently." This almost mysterious quiet—a softening that is immediately apparent—is much in evidence here.

The vernacular houses of the immediate area are white with steep, simple roofs. Nearby, at the end of a long pier, is a century-old boathouse whose form speaks of its simple practicality.

The Blumenthal House faces the water, its similar forms shifting in relation to one another in an attempt to reduce its size by breaking up its massing while reflecting the interior function of each pavilion. The absence of overhangs, gutters, and trim abstracts the local 19th-century houses through a more deliberate and expressed linear restraint.

For the most part, the interior spaces follow the forms of the roofs and are opened with "finger skylights"— long, narrow openings in the roof that allow the sun to enter the all-white interiors and trace its unexpected path across the floors and walls. All of the openings are either fixed glass windows or sliding-glass pocket doors. The wall pockets that hold the doors also contain screened doors and oak shutters with fixed louvers.

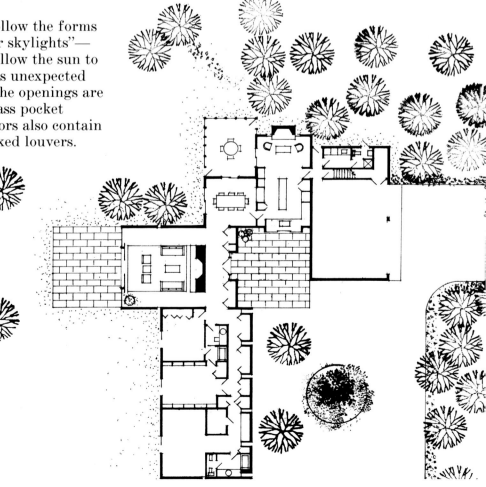

Opposite. The living room, split
chimney mass, and skylight.

Above. An open pocket door,
concealing sash, screen, and
louvered shutter.

# House in the Virgin Islands

*Estate Carlton, St. Croix*

The south coast of St. Croix is rocky, arid, and windy, and when the trade winds are not blowing, it can be a warm and rather humid place. The site of this all-white, stucco house on the south coast is very close to the edge of a sharp coral cliff, 10 feet above the surf. The proximity of the sea here is as exhilarating as the colors of the Caribbean are enchanting.

The house and its guest house present all-glass facades to the sea, their 17-foot heights protected by detached wind- and sunscreens. The roof and the surrounding terrace catch the rainwater that is stored in large underground cisterns. When approached by land, the house and its walls totally block out the sea. Tall trees, planted just outside the walls, promise relief at the end of a journey across the near-desert landscape.

The house is penetrated by a roofless passage into a large, sunscreened court that opens onto every room in the house. The beneficent climate allows this open courtyard, with its large ficus tree, to serve as a sort of interior town square, a space through which all must pass. Meals are often served in the court, as well as by the pool, in the dining room, or in the lee of one of the six windscreens. There are four bedrooms plus staff quarters in the main house; a smaller detached house is reserved for guests.

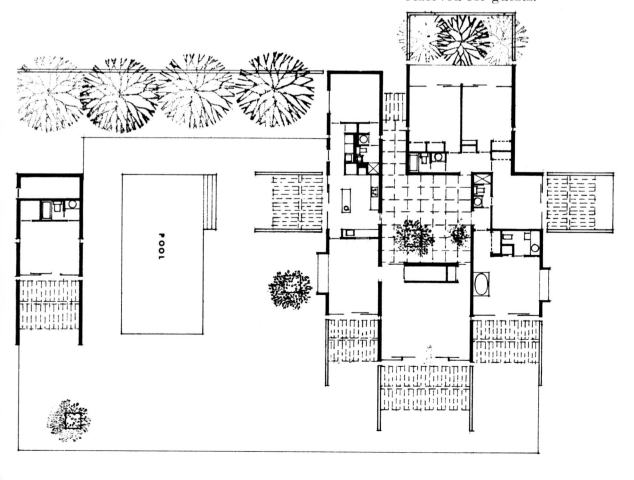

POOL

Top. The house as seen from the guest house.

Bottom. The pool terrace.
Opposite. The central court.

# Jacobsen House

*Georgetown, Washington, D.C.*

Located on a shaded street lined with brick sidewalks, this early-19th-century house was originally a two-story, red-brick, Federal-style structure with two dormers facing the street. Records in the Georgetown Public Library state that a third floor was added in 1871, and that the whole was made "tasteful" by the addition of an Italianate cornice and bay window facing the street. It is believed that the brick was painted a sandstone color at that time, in keeping with the popular Italianate style of the day.

The small garden to the left of the house was walled in to form a forecourt when the house was altered and added onto in 1968. The original front entry was demoted to kitchen door, and the pedimented trim, entry light, and address plate were removed. The new front entry is concealed from the street, revealing itself only after one enters through a gate (where the entry light and address plate now reside). The ivy-covered forecourt is formed by the original house, the forecourt wall, and the new and nearly windowless two-story addition that stretches across the width of the property behind the original portion of the house.

The surprise of a Georgetown house is often its garden. One enters this house at close to absolute center; the major axis extends through the center of the dining room's 1871 bay window on the street, continues through the new living room bay, and reaches beyond to the garden. The garden facade abstracts 19th-century fenestration with 20th-century detailing. The garden itself consists only of a stone terrace, a bank of English ivy, and, at the rear, 15 columnar American holly trees planted in two matching rows. Cool and evergreen, the trees are individually lit at night to erase interior reflections on the 10-foot-high sections of glass. The eye is drawn to the garden by day as well as at night, and the axial sight lines allow the garden view to be enjoyed from dining room, library, and living room alike.

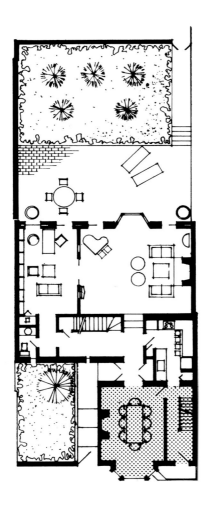

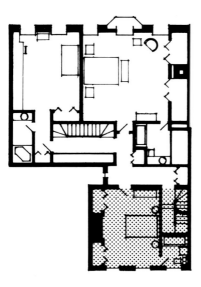

Opposite. The library with eggcrate bookcases.

Above. A view from the living room toward the library. The painting on the wall is by Anne Truitt.

# Schwaikert House

*Northwestern Connecticut*

The rolling site of this house includes a lake with a
small island and a view over the water to the Berkshire
Mountains beyond. Lichen-covered outcroppings of
tough stone appear throughout this ancient and
beautiful countryside. Tall pines stand close to gnarled
oaks and lacy hemlocks, and white strings of silver
birch brighten the deepest of shadows.

The house is situated close to a rock that is very large.
The staggered pavilions completely conceal the lake
and the view across the calm, reflecting water until one
is well into the living room. A large wood deck nearly
equaling the area of the house extends its space and its
activities. The massive chimney of local black stone is
divided into two shafts, announcing the entry. Every
room in the house—save the bathrooms—has a view of
the lake. The clerestory just below the ridge line of
each roof reflects light across the ceiling plane,
washing all of the interiors with soft, natural
illumination. The second floor, reached by a spiral
stair, includes three boys' bedrooms. The parents' room
at the far end enjoys both a view of the lake and a
framed view over a small waterfall of the freshwater
swimming pool that was cut out of solid rock.

Clad in red cypress, the building has been left to
weather to a series of verticals that range in color from
deep gray to quiet silver. The garden was designed by
the architect.

# The Renwick Gallery

*Washington, D.C.*

The history of this remarkable building was the primary consideration when the Renwick Gallery was returned to its original use, a full century after its construction. It began as a picture gallery, housing the contemporary European genre paintings collected by William Wilson Corcoran. In 1859, Corcoran retained architect James Renwick to design his picture gallery for a site on Pennsylvania Avenue. Apparently influenced by Hector Lefuel's recently completed work on the Louvre, Renwick managed with credible skill to manipulate the scale of the truly grand and monumental Pavilion de Flore and design a building appropriate for a prominent corner site in America's capital city.

The building received little attention until the early 1960s, when it was included as part of the restoration program for nearby Lafayette Square initiated by President and Mrs. John F. Kennedy. With the exception of the front entry, work on the Renwick's exterior was completed by architect John Carl Warnecke in 1968. It was then, under the direction and inspiration of S. Dillon Ripley, secretary of the Smithsonian Institution, that this small building with its great rooms was given new life and definition as an art museum.

Requirements for air-conditioning, elevators, toilets, and even drinking fountains threatened the effort to re-create the interiors of this historic building. To "evoke the spirit" of James Renwick, great care was taken to mask all evidence of 20th-century intrusion. Elevator, restrooms, and telephones were gathered and relegated to "shadow" spaces, and actually "painted out" in a very dark brown. The interior spaces had been partitioned and subdivided; these nonoriginal walls were removed, along with hanging fluorescent fixtures, boxlike closets, and other incursions, until the original spaces were revealed. The original colors and *faux* patterns of both wood and marble were researched and painstakingly re-created. Particular attention was paid to contemporary lighting that would enhance, and not intrude upon, the spirit of the spaces. It is this spirit of the James Renwick spaces that carries the day.

# Baker House

*Frederick, Maryland*

The thick dark forest of oak around this house claims half the side of a mountain in western Maryland. The site was graded to produce a broad shelf that would serve as a podium to hold the house. The isolation of the site freed the design of all contextual constraints other than those imposed by nature. The brick and its trim are painted white; their brightness announces these light-filled forms in the middle of the wood.

The formality of the plan, with its three pavilions diagonally linked at their corners, clearly expresses the individual purposes of the pavilions—public (living), private (sleeping), and utility (garage, laundry). The pyramidal roof forms are topped with glass-roofed cupolas that bring light into the central space within each pavilion. In both the public and private pavilions, the cupolas help to define atriums that serve as a surprising arboretum in one and a light-filled, nearly monumental playroom surrounded by children's bedrooms in the other. All of the floors are surfaced in local slate, which helps to extend the spaces joining pavilion to pavilion. The diagonal lines, so evident in plan, carry the eye from space to space inside the house. The strong diagonals are accented by the ridge lines that fall from the cupola to the corners in each pavilion, and then rise again to the light of the cupola in the adjoining pavilion.

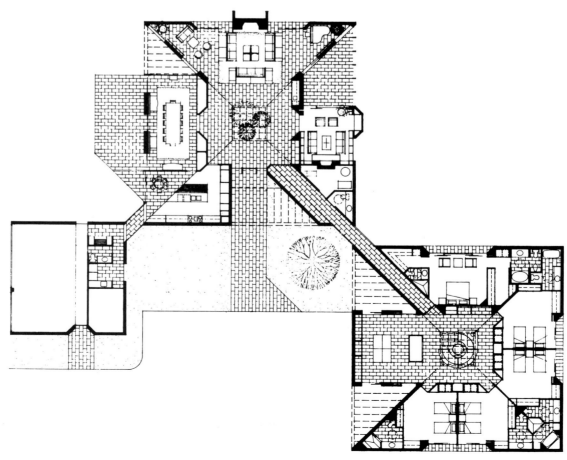

Opposite. The atrium as seen from the front door. The living room lies beyond the trees; the eggcrate coffers give access to the skylight above.

Top. The living room.
Bottom. Atrium in public pavilion serves as playroom.

# Arts and Industries Building

*Washington, D.C.*

In restoring the front facade, central rotunda, and
four radiating halls of the Smithsonian Institution's
Arts and Industries Building in Washington, the
challenge was to recapture the essence of the original
building without falling into a hackneyed imitation of
the past.

Construction of what was originally called the National
Museum was completed in 1881, in time for the
building to serve as the site of the Inaugural Ball
given for President James Garfield. The structure
was designed to house the many exhibits given to
the nation during the 1876 Centennial Exposition in
Philadelphia. By the middle of this century, however,
careful restoration was long overdue, and the planned
installation of a Bicentennial exhibition made it vital.

With help from Assistant Secretary for Museum
Programs Paul Perrot and the Smithsonian's Office
of Facilities Planning and Engineering Services,
Engineering and Design Branch, the period to which
the interior should be restored was determined.
Samples discovered under layers of paint proved that
the walls had been painted an ochre shade, which was
reintroduced. Over the arches, stencils similar to those
depicted in old drawings and photographs were
applied, their colors determined after extensive
reading of contemporary correspondence in the
Smithsonian's archives. The light fixtures specified
closely reproduced the gas chandeliers used in the 1876
Centennial buildings in Philadelphia. A Victorian
fountain was installed as the focus of the rotunda. A
new encaustic tile floor was designed and installed—
a particularly formidable task, since its method of
production was universally abandoned in the
mid-1930s.

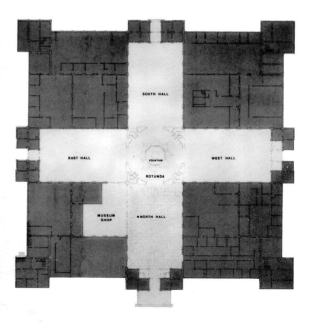

# Three Linked Pavilions

*Washington, D.C.*

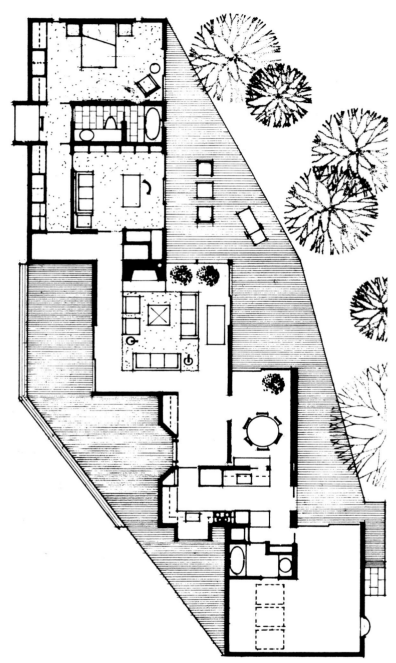

The average American house is somewhere around 1,980 square feet in area. This house, built for a retired couple on the last vacant lot in an established residential neighborhood of Washington, D.C., is exactly that size. Its triangular site—used as a fill-dump by the builders of the adjacent houses—falls off abruptly at one edge. The site's irregular shape, the proximity of neighboring houses, and the clients' desire for a one-story house on a lot with a 34-foot grade change were among the challenges of this project.

To take advantage of the topography, the entry grade was extended with a raised deck. The openings are oriented to avoid sight lines to neighboring houses, so that the views across the decks take in only the treetops. The unmistakable "house" shape presented by the front facade reflects a conscious effort to obey the existing scale of the neighborhood; the staggered massing relates to the property line. The front facade preserves privacy from the street, but it also fulfills the clients' request for an observation window. The secluded entrance is reached by a drive and deck on the northern side.

The clients' program called for a skylit painting studio that could double as an extra bedroom and bath; and for a library; a master bedroom; and living, cooking, and dining areas. High triangular transoms admit soft, reflected light into each pavilion. Storage and mechanical space is provided in the high-ceilinged basement beneath the rear portion of the house. The basement can be accessed from the outside and through a counterweighted trap door in the living room floor.

The house, as seen from the
street.

A view of the house and its deck,
from below.

The wood deck with access to all
four pavilions.

The living room and the deck,
beyond.

The dining room and a view into
the living room.

# Elliott House

*Chevy Chase, Maryland*

The street here is nearly everything. The tall elms that line both sides of this street are reinforced with proud houses that reflect not only the romantic periods of domestic architecture, but also a distinctly American type of neighborhood that is rapidly being replaced. There is a strong sense of nostalgia here, and it speaks to us about the dark potentials of change. This pleasant street still echoes with the cries of playing children, the banging of screen doors, and the hush of the first snow.

The original portion of this house was built in 1871 as an outbuilding for a larger house of similar style. The main house was lost long ago with a change in the street plan, but the smaller one survived the fever of subdivision and the onslaught of popular taste. The owners bought the house in 1975—in spite of its turquoise exterior. The original entry and front porch were removed. A floor-to-ceiling bay window was substituted, and then repeated on the new wing that expanded the area of house by nearly 50 percent.

As a result of the neighborhood's subdivision, the house lacked the traditional backyard. For this reason, the owners, after living in the house for almost 10 years, asked that a gazebo be designed to provide them with a place for outside dining and yet preserve their outdoor privacy. The gazebo was designed in the true spirit of a folly—as a place to go when one is feeling out of sorts. Its style is far more flamboyant and intricate than the relatively quiet Queen Anne style of the main house. Yet its wishbone truss, polychrome trim, fishscale shingles, and other details recalling the architectural lexicon of the late 19th century seem altogether appropriate for this house—and this street.

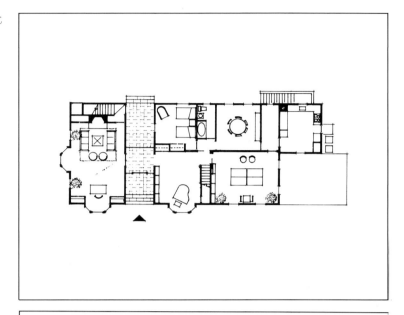

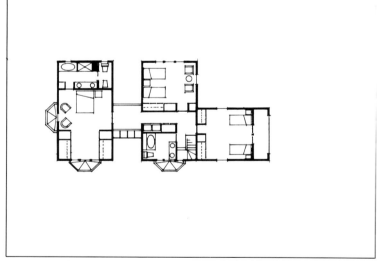

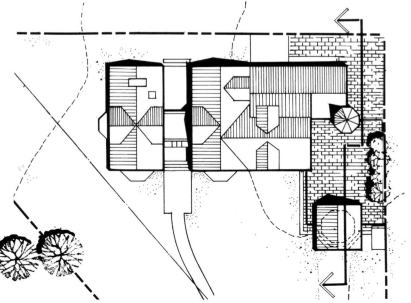

Opposite. The new living room.    Above. The new bay, as seen
from the living room.

# American College of Greece Gymnasium and Library

*Athens, Greece*

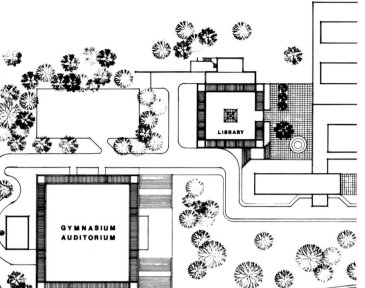

On the slope of the mountain chain that forms the southern edge of the Plain of Attica sits the campus of the American College of Greece, designed by the Greek architect Constantine Doxiadis in the late 1950s. The two buildings presented here, a library and a gymnasium, were designed to respectfully join this gathering of concrete post-and-beam buildings established by Doxiadis.

The library was given a place of distinction in the master plan. A plaza was designed as a buffer between the library and the existing campus. It holds a small amphitheater and pieces of sculpture by the distinguished Greek sculptor Takis. The plaza also provides an isolated and privileged setting for the freestanding, 28-meter-square building. The perimeters of the library are glazed with floor-to-ceiling tinted glass protected from the Greek sunlight by continuous sunscreens of precast concrete. The column-free interior is lit by a central skylight that floods the space with filtered light and announces the monumental stairs linking the almost identical upper and lower levels.

The natural terrain of the site was used to deliberate design advantage. Grading allowed the gymnasium to fit into the hill and appear small next to its more important immediate neighbor, the library. Growing taller as its entrance stairs descend the grade, the largest building on campus appears to be a one-story, glass-walled building when viewed from the two-story library. Only after one goes down the stairs and reaches the midway point at the entry/playing-floor level is the five-story mass of the gymnasium revealed. The elegant great room seats 2,500 people.

Above. The library at plaza level
with open stacks.
Below. First-floor plan.

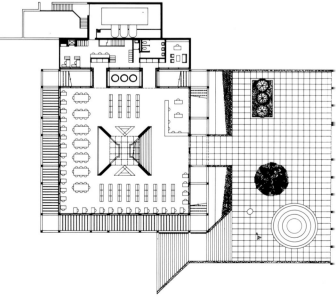

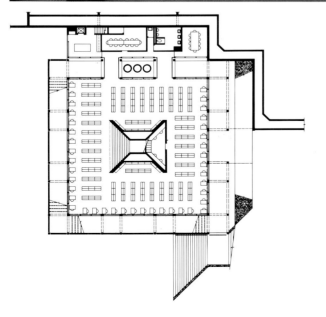

Left. The monumental central stair.
Right. The expressed HVAC ductwork on the lower level.
Below. Lower-level floor plan.

The gymnasium entry and broad
exterior stair.

The dance and exercise room
beneath the rake of gym seating.
The glass wall overlooks a grove
of pines.

Above. The playing floor,
arranged for graduation
ceremonies.
Below. A section.

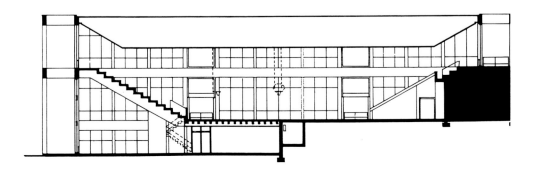

# Dixon House

*Long Lake, Minnesota*

Situated in northern Minnesota, this house was conceived as a rural farm cluster that would have southern views to a scenic lake across a broad expanse of sloping land. The main house, guest house, and garage are grouped symmetrically around an informal courtyard; a six-foot wooden retaining wall to the north completes the enclosure.

The approach to the house was designed to present a series of revelations and surprises. One approaches via the driveway through a straight tunnel of trees; when the drive breaks out into an open meadow, the silhouette of the house and garage suddenly appear. As the visitor proceeds into the forecourt through the narrow space between the buildings, the glass entry is revealed to beckon and welcome. Once the visitor is through the door, the broad glass wall of the living room reveals for the first time a panoramic view of the lake.

The structures adapt the coloring of the black barns common to the region. But since there is no color in nature that is purely white, there can be no color that is purely black; depending on the light, these exterior walls vary from deep purple through cool gray to warm brown.

The design and particularly the detailing express a very taut skin on the exterior, so the white, high-ceilinged volumes within underscore the tension formed by the intersections of white interior and black exterior at the glazing line. Because of the deep overhangs, no gutters or downspouts are required; thus, where the house turns from black to white, the detailing is razor-sharp.

SEVANUSA 6·78

Below. Plan of main house, guest house, garage, pool, and courtyard with linden trees.

Opposite. Black and white living room with glass wall and slitted-roof skylight to admit sunlight.

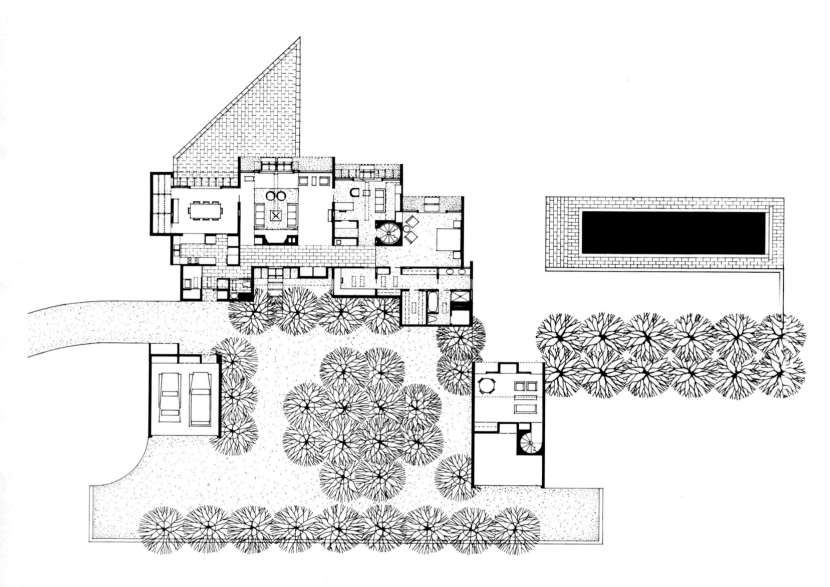

# Challinor House

*Southern Connecticut*

This house is at the edge of a broad, green lawn that addresses the full sweep of Long Island Sound. It is surrounded by a family of 19th-century houses, and when viewed from any of the ever-present sailboats that beat about the sound, this five-part abstraction of a neoclassic house appears to be a member of the family.

The Palladian plan of the all-cedar house rests near one edge of a broad wood podium whose entire circumference is defined by near-monumental stairs that adjust themselves down the gentle slope toward the water.

The central pavilion's pedimental ends are glazed. One end casts additional light against the interior roof plane in the rather formal living room. The other is the dramatic, single source of natural light in a second-story guest room over the entry. In addition to the guest room and three bedrooms indicated on the plan, the second floor of one wing also contains a large dormitory space.

The conscientious owners annually wash down the one-inch-by-four-inch, tongue-and-groove, vertical cedar exterior siding with bleach so that the wood retains its beautiful silver tones, which enhance the temple-like facades. Because of the dark green hill immediately inland from the house, the structure appears white when seen from the sound, which adds considerably to the intended trompe l'oeil of its neoclassicism.

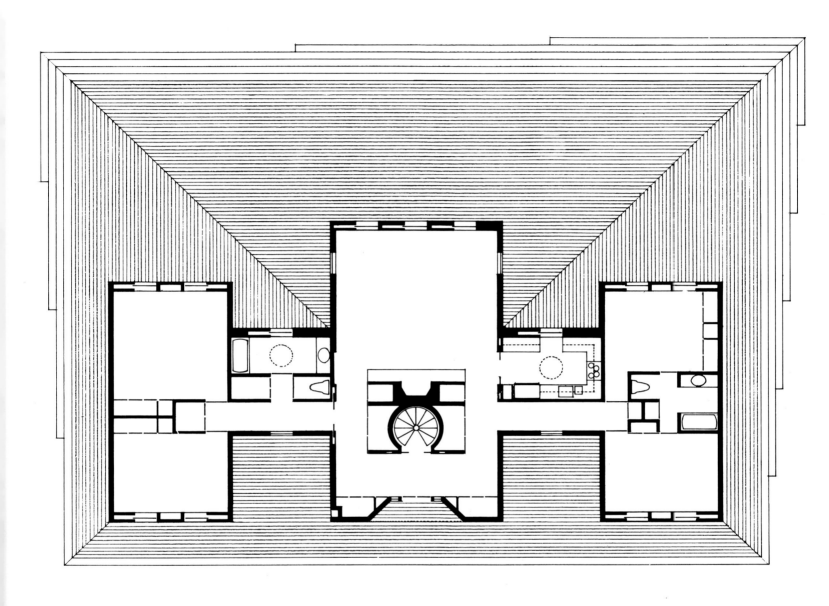

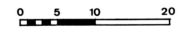

# Putterman House

*Central Pennsylvania*

The rural site of this large house and studio for a prominent American artist was chosen because it was close to the artist's friends, but the site and scale of the neighboring houses presented serious problems with continuity and "good manners."

Reflecting the gable ends of the small houses lining the street, this long horizontal house with four gabled pavilions aligns itself behind a grove of existing pine trees. Different functions are housed in separate pavilions, with the pavilions joined together by skylit galleries in which the owner's collection of American art is displayed. The studio and workshop wing takes up much of the square footage of the house for the processing, printing, and storing of lithographs, etchings, photographs, and paintings. The large deck is a device that visually erases the roofs of the neighboring houses on the downhill side of the site, so that spectacular views of the Susquehanna Valley can be enjoyed from nearly every room in the house.

The street facade presents only the glazed gable ends above a long white wall that is penetrated by a single opening. The opening announces a disarming entry, on axis with the tall, twin chimneys that reach high above the parallel ridges of the aligned roofs. The entry opens onto a long hall connecting all four pavilions and serving as both a light-filled gallery and as a "street" that links the various elements of the plan. The broad deck surrounds a swimming pool, the mirrored surface of which reflects light onto the ceiling planes of the nearby pavilions. The long wall facing the street manages to maintain the surrounding domestic scale; equally as vital, it withholds the long view until the visitor is within.

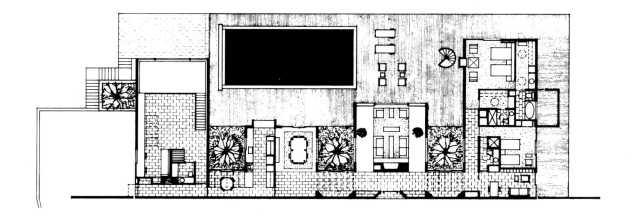

# Buckwalter House

*Eastern Pennsylvania*

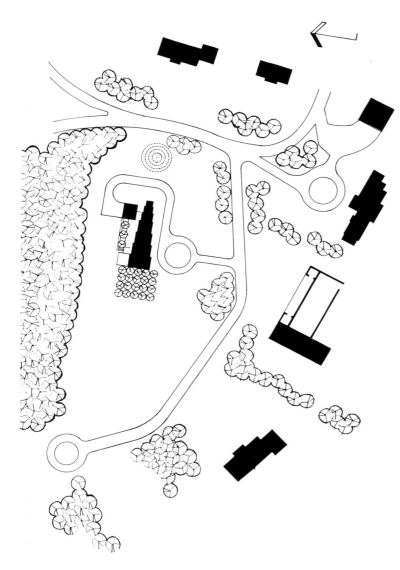

The "telescope house" was common to this part of Pennsylvania, especially in the utopian communities that gathered here more than a century ago. Increments were traditionally added as families grew, with each successive addition made to the gable end of its predecessor, repeating the proportions but reducing the size.

The site is reached after a mile-long drive along a private road lined with houses reflecting period and romantic influences on domestic architecture. The owners of these houses, soon to become neighbors, clearly wanted the new house to preserve the historic character and domestic scale of the area's architecture.

The design of this house abstracts 18th- and 19th-century "telescope" traditions. Each of the seven units descends in height and diminishes in width in regular reductions of two feet on each side. This reduction in size permitted the fitting of mirrored, insulating glass in the exposed walls of each of the adjoining larger units. The reflective quality of the glass allows daytime privacy and conserves energy; the glass surrounds also admit natural light and provide surprising glimpses of the out-of-doors.

Each unit of the house reflects a specific use: living room; three-story entry foyer and circulation; library/dining room; kitchen; laundry/mudroom; and workshop.

The largest gable end is completely glazed, exposing a steel-reinforced balloon frame that expresses both modern and historical design technologies. A grove of 36 dogwood trees, planted like an orchard, faces the reflective glass of the tall gable end. But there appear to be 72 dogwoods because of their mirrored reflections. At night, each tree can be lit by a recessed fixture in the grass beneath, activating the reflections and turning the tall, mirrored wall into an unpenetrable reflective surface; when the outside is dark, the wall becomes transparent and the balloon frame is revealed.

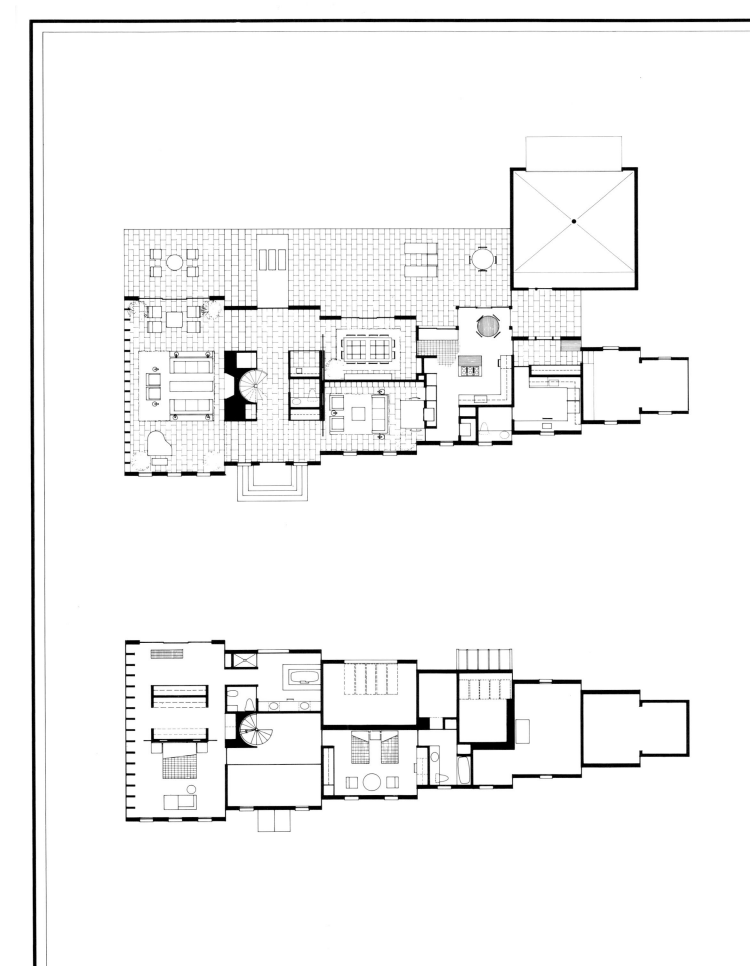

# House in Kentucky

*Lexington*

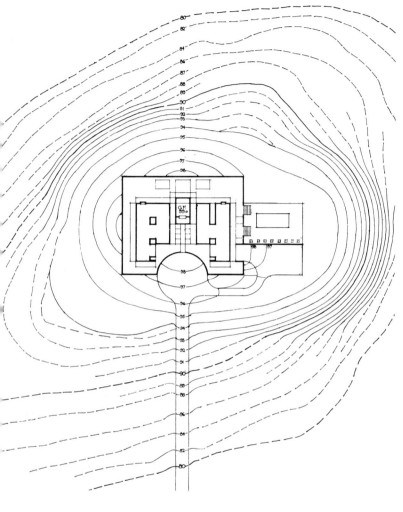

This house sits on a bluegrass hill—one of the many that make up this horse farm of 1,000 acres. Because of the substrata of limestone beneath these gentle hills, the grass here is astonishingly thick, lush, and—yes—actually blue-green.

The vernacular architecture in these environs is typically brick, painted white; the local clays aren't sufficiently resistant for the sometimes severe winters, so bricks have traditionally been painted or sealed with whitewash. The houses of the old plantations and of today's famous stud farms are, for the most part, classical revivals whose pedimental facades are supported by round, white, painted-brick columns.

The site and the indigenous architecture combined to evoke strong esthetic and historic themes during the design of this house, which is an abstraction of the South's familiar columned "house on the hill."

The post-and-beam construction was expressed by maintaining the integrity of the column: Aside from the Roman travertine on which they rest and the wooden sunscreens or rafters that they support, the columns contact only glass. The large expanses of glass that define the views from every room are shielded by deep sunscreens on the exterior. The same details are expressed in the interior as skylights.

The house crowns its hill, and was deliberately placed on a podium of white painted brick to separate it from the green of the meadow. The podium is punctured with silver birch trees; when lit at night, the trees erase interior reflections on the glass and allow the columns to frame evening views that are as tranquil as those observable during the day. The architect designed the landscape.

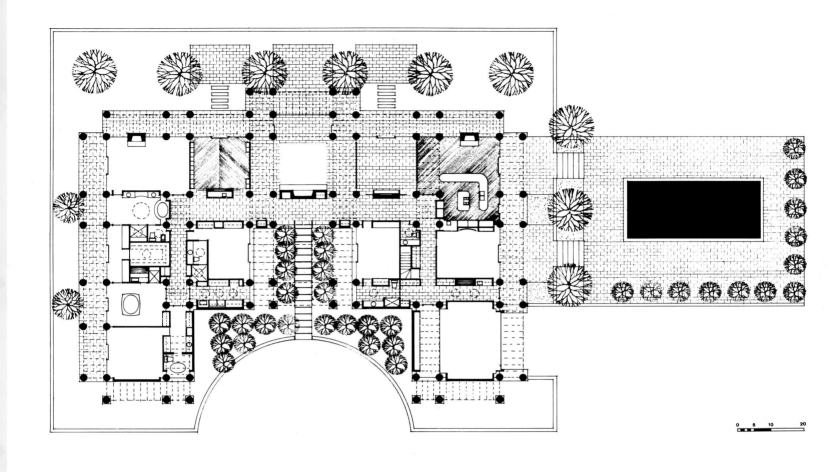

# Gettysburg College Library

*Gettysburg, Pennsylvania*

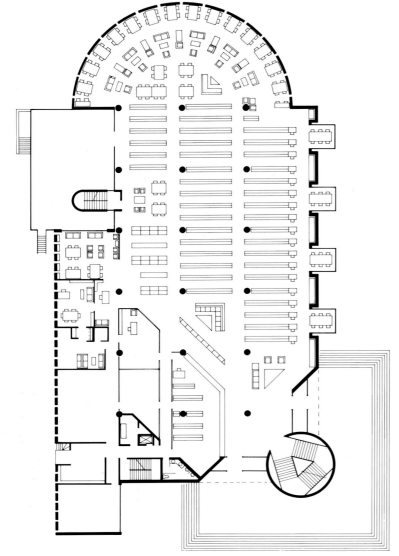

The charming campus of this distinguished liberal arts college in southern Pennsylvania is a polite gathering of late-19th-century academic buildings. It is dominated by the Romanesque tower of a century-old classroom building whose palette of materials, massing, and architectural order formed the vocabulary for the college's new library.

Built of burgundy brick and matching rustication, the new building, like its inspiration, has a tower, bay windows, a matching roof, and an apsidal end. Although the new Musselman Library is actually larger, the 1880 building continues to dominate the campus through a manipulation of the new building's scale; it is difficult to determine the size of the new library without the presence of a human figure.

The architectural elements that announce the size of the Romanesque building were abstracted and altered on the new building to maintain the established order. The new brick and colored mortar match the old building's, and the precast masonry trim was detailed to complement the textures and colors of other existing campus structures. The canted base on which the main block of the library rests is also a reflection of the older building. The new tower is now a focal point on campus, its base a large, raised plaza that serves as a gathering place for students.

Inside is the library's collection of 450,000 volumes, the majority available in open stacks beneath the great slate roof. The mechanical spaces occupy the attic. The library can accommodate 800 readers scattered throughout the building in the 12 large window bays or in the large apsidal reading room.

Opposite. The entrance podium and the tower.

Below. The triangular monumental stair that occupies the tower.

# House on the Eastern Shore

*Maryland*

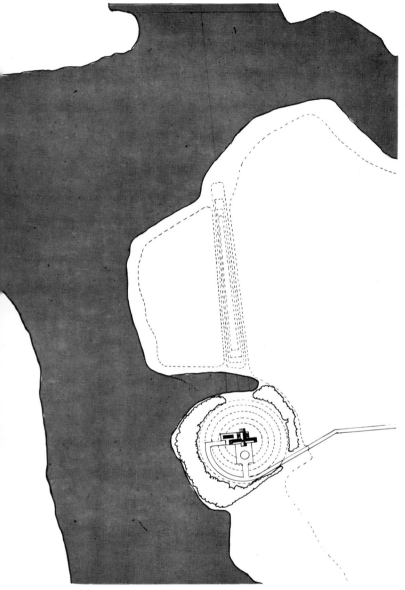

The Eastern Shore of Maryland is flat, edged with countless coves, and threaded by streams and rivers that flow to the Chesapeake Bay. The houses of those who work the land and water here are generally white and wood-frame with quiet traces of the Gothic Revival. All are readily visible either from the land or from the water, but rarely from both. The great plantation houses of the 18th century presented their most imposing facades to the water, from which quarter the more prestigious members of society could be expected to approach. Nineteenth-century houses, built as roads and transportation improved, generally anticipated a landward approach and turned their best faces to that front. Like most of the neighboring homes, this residence can be seen from some distance away. As one drives along the country roads, its white buildings stand bright amid the rich green fields and the almost black trunks of the trees.

The house is on a knoll created with the earth that was carved out to form the allée approach to the house. The allée is 600 yards long and reinforces the major axis of the cruciform plan of the house. As can be seen from the site plan, there is an axial focus from the living room south toward the river and the bay beyond; this same axis also aligns the allée and the entry of the house.

The basic elements of the surrounding vernacular architecture are all present here: a formal plan, multiple gables (each with an oculus), tall chimneys, tall windows, trellised terraces, and ample porches. The abstraction of these historical forms allowed the house to become a part of the quiet scene, to share in a sense of belonging.

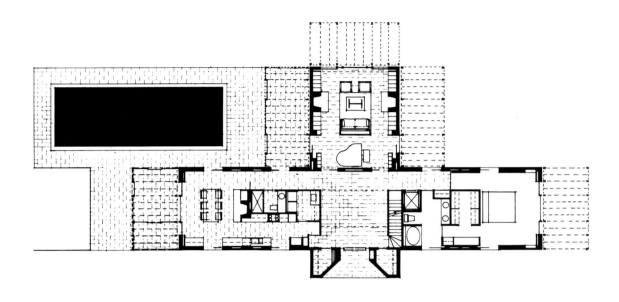

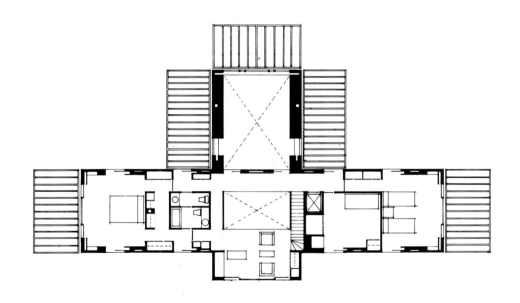

# The Library for the American University in Cairo

*Cairo, Egypt*

The American University in Cairo is a U.S.-accredited, liberal arts university located on Tahrir Square in the heart of this vibrant, bustling city. The downtown campus is an oasis of peace and academe amid the dust and noise that swirl around it. The challenge in designing its new library was to filter out the sounds and the air of the city, and at the same time place a cool, green, interior garden at the library's center.

The entrance, a tall portal reminiscent of the entrances to Mamluk mosques, is located on a corner and addresses the gate of the main campus half a block away. The street facades, which are closed and reflect the neighboring buildings in scale and materials, stand in sharp contrast to the courtyard elevations of floor-to-ceiling glass with their play of light, shade, and shadow.

Entering off the hot and crowded street, one reaches the tree-filled garden after passing through a wide pedestrian tunnel, beneath a foot bridge (which serves the library entrance one level above) and up broad stairs to a raised plaza. Here the library is revealed. Four levels of floor-to-ceiling glass expose the garden to the entire library's interior space. The bridge points toward the main desk and card catalogs; the stacks stand free and accessible. The large expanse of glass is protected from the Egyptian sun by a sunscreen, which squares off the "bite" in the plan that opens the interiors to the welcome, cool, reflected green light of the garden.

To keep this open-stack library as open and flexible as possible, the massive (six feet on a side) triangular columns are located on the perimeter of the building, supporting beams with clear spans of 88 feet. The reading rooms and stacks occupy three floors, with the technical and support functions located in a partially recessed lower level. The ceilings are a black aluminum eggcrate, and nonmodular lighting allows the librarian flexibility to rearrange the collection as it grows.

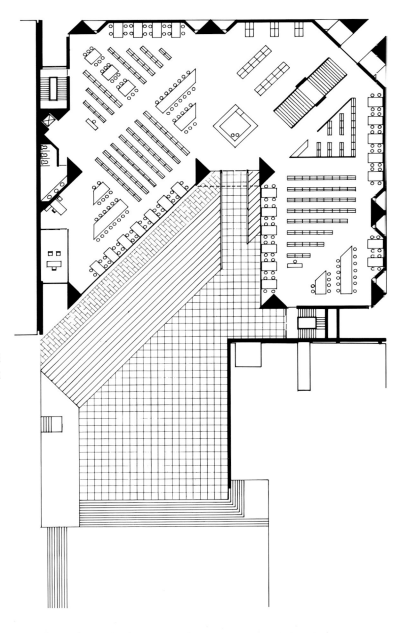

Top. Entry to the second campus through the corner of the library.

Bottom. The entrance plaza serves as a reflecting plane that lights the library, beyond.

# Athens College Theater

*Athens, Greece*

The U.S. Department of State's Agency for International Development provided the funds that enabled this distinguished private preparatory school—founded in 1925 and headed by an American—to meet its long-established need for a theater.

The campus occupies a rare, wooded site in suburban Athens. It is dominated by a large and beloved neoclassic building that houses not only the majority of the classrooms but the very spirit of the school as well. The site selected for the new theater was a dense grove of pines directly adjacent to this grand classical pile.

It was intended that the new 850-seat theater play a secondary role to its neoclassic neighbor, so its design takes advantage of the terrain; the rake of the seating follows the grade, with the stage well below grade at the rear of the site, and the roof a modest 15 feet in height at the entry.

The circular house is surrounded by an art gallery on both levels in the square plan. The walls and floors of theater and gallery alike are covered with carpet for better acoustics. All four elevations of the building are similar. The suggested and elongated proscenium reveals the glass entries to the gallery on three facades. The fourth facade allows the stagehouse and fly to emerge from the confines of the square.

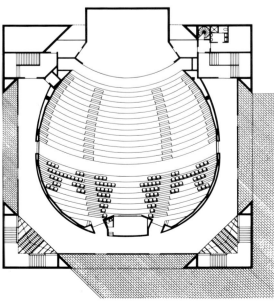

173

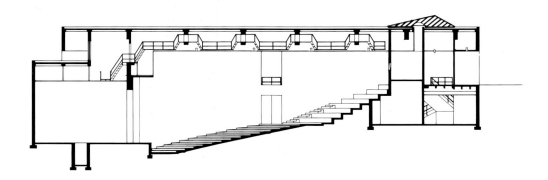

# Huge House

*McLean, Virginia*

To withhold the full impact of this spectacular site high above the Potomac River until one is inside the house, two walls were built parallel to the cliff's edge above the river's first major cataract, some 200 feet below. One wall, 13 feet tall, runs from the east property line to the front entry. The other wall, 11 feet high, runs from the edge of a ravine on the west to a point 20 feet beyond the entry and 8 feet away from its parallel counterpart. Behind these two solid walls, all of the facades that form the two-level house are floor-to-ceiling insulating glass.

The swimming pool and its terrace are at a 90-degree angle to the major axis of the house and are screened by a third wall expressing this outdoor enclosure of space. Two allées were carved through the woods down the cliff to provide views of the rapids in all seasons. A curved wall screens an outdoor shower and cabana at the end of the pool, reflecting the wall at the end of the house.

The large cylinder near the center of the plan and on axis with the entry door serves as a visual core or pivot. Wrapped in bookcases on the entry floor, the cylinder defines the separate zones of the open plan. It houses the main stairway to the bedrooms on the lower level; on both levels, it contains baths, fireplaces, and flues. Every room in the house enjoys the spectacle of the Potomac cataract far below. The change of seasons, a shared and glorious event for most of us, becomes a participatory rite in this glass house.

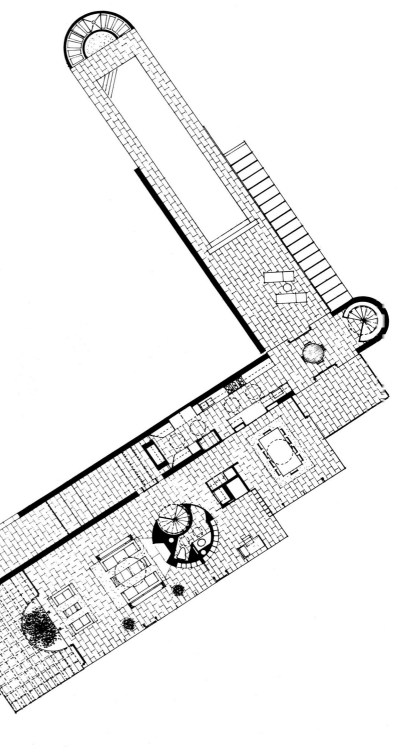

# University of Michigan Alumni Center

*Ann Arbor, Michigan*

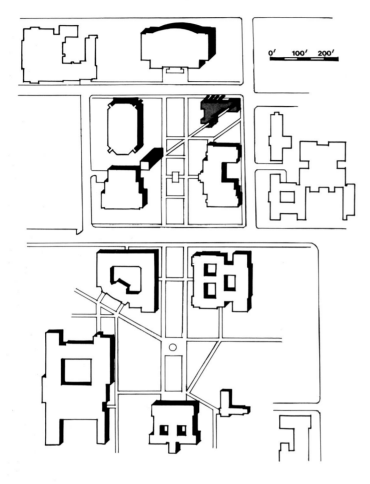

The Alumni Center is located at the very heart of this vast midwestern campus. The site is surrounded on all four sides by buildings of monumental scale, arranged parallel to the major axis that forms the central mall of the campus. For more than a century, students have walked across this site as a matter of rite. Their traditional pathway is respected in the design scheme and is expressed symbolically and physically as a device to bring the students closer to the alumni.

A desire to abstract the stylistic elements of the nearby buildings strongly influenced the form and choice of materials. The Alumni Center's immediate neighbor to the south is a venerable brick and limestone-banded, collegiate Tudor building erected in the 1920s. Matching brick, limestone string coursing, and repetitive gable ends were called for on the new building to emphasize its contextual association with, and responsibility to, the old. However, the detailing is hard-edged, and the vocabulary that establishes the scale of the neighboring building has clearly been manipulated in this process of historical abstraction.

The new building is basically a series of flexible meeting rooms, surrounded and topped by the many offices that support the multifaceted programs of the Alumni Association. The structure is a steel frame with brick and limestone veneers; the roofing is factory-coated metal. The large meeting room on the ground floor is served by four fireplaces. The walls are surfaced in blue carpet trimmed with brass strips. The great room is capable of being subdivided into four 18-by-28-foot rooms, each enjoying one of the fireplaces; the movable dividing walls are identical to the permanent walls.

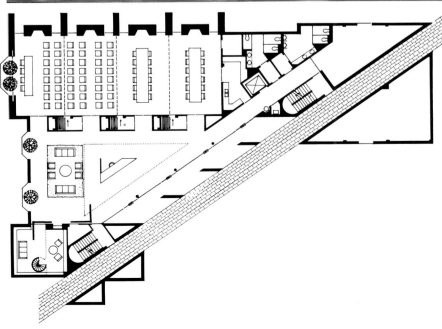

Top. The tall chimneys equal the height—and suggest the mass—of the Modern Language building across the mall.

Bottom. The gables reflect the stylistic vocabulary of the majority of the campus buildings.

Above. The reception hall as "town square."

Opposite. The great hall can seat 300 or be divided into four 18-foot-wide conference rooms. It focuses on a large fireplace and enjoys 22-foot ceilings.

# Zamoiski House

*Eastern Shore, Maryland*

Located in the Tidewater region of Maryland's Eastern Shore, this four-pavilion house with outbuildings is used for long weekends and throughout most of the summer. Because of its exposure and isolation, the building's primarily glass skin is protected when the house is unoccupied by floor-to-ceiling shutters that are operated by electrically driven winches. When the owner is gone, the entire exterior is sealed, protecting the house from storms and vandalism. When the house is occupied and the shutters are in a horizontal position, they serve as sunscreens, their adjustable louvers capable of casting interesting light patterns as their shade reduces the heat load inside the house. One of the outbuildings serves as an outdoor kitchen/buffet, servicing the swimming pool; the other, near the parking area, is for tools and storage.

The house is sited to reduce its apparent size, as seen from the water, and to take maximum advantage of both primary and secondary views. In addition to the living room's view of the Chesapeake Bay, the other pavilions share closer, more intimate views of the site's freshwater pond. A double row of columnar cedars reinforces the visual strength of the drive and screens the house on the parallel-axis approach.

The residence is wood-frame; clapboard siding was milled to match the module of the adjustable, louvered shutters. The interior flooring and terrace are Pennsylvania bluestone; the roof, black asphalt shingle. All fixed and operable openings are double-glazed, with the paired exceptions defining the outside corners of the living room. Each of the four pavilions is heated and cooled with a geothermal heat-pump system located in its attic.

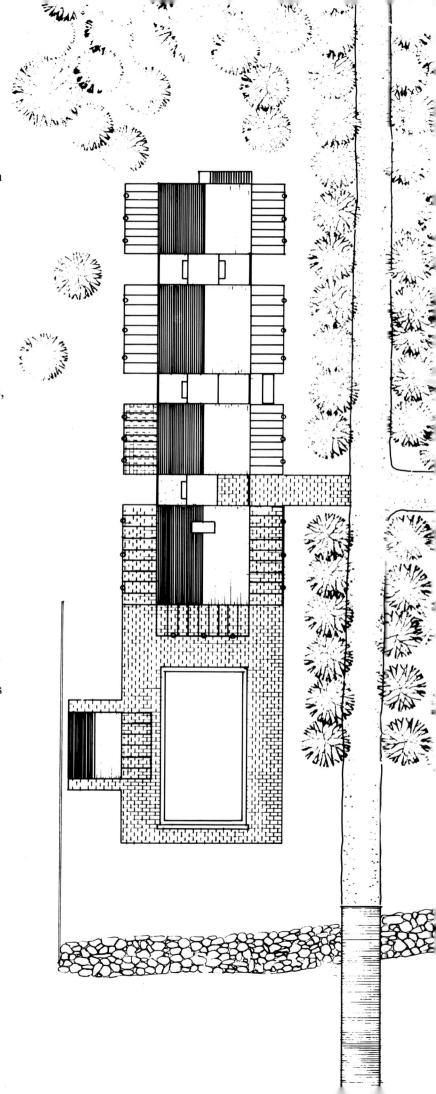

Top. The front door and living-room pavilion.

Bottom. The facades, including the living room on the right, overlook the freshwater pond.

# Alumni Square, Georgetown University

*Georgetown, Washington, D.C.*

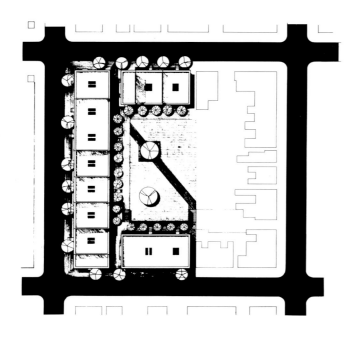

This site occupies half of a residential block in a historic district of Washington, D.C. Across the street is Georgetown University's main classroom building, a 19th-century Gothic structure listed in the National Register. The surrounding streets are lined with late-19th-century brick row houses that quietly speak of their Italianate influence and aspirations.

The steeply sloped site, which falls 22 feet from north to south, encouraged the massing to be stepped and allowed the large dormitories to be designed as small "row houses." The broken rooflines define individual units. Because the street is domestic in scale—with brick, sandstone, wood trim, and iron fencing the primary materials—the use of brick in the dormitory complex expresses a sense of belonging as well as respect for the existing structures. The brick detailing and coursing reinforce the close association of the new buildings and their historic context. The "row houses" reflect the low-scale Italianate style that came to dominate this neighborhood in the 1880s. The facades generally present a restrained appearance, except for the deliberately overscaled cornices and oriel windows that were abstracted from nearby predecessors.

One of the university's requirements was that these 90 units be readily convertible into private housing, so each of the four-student apartments was equipped with a built-in kitchen. In addition, the U-shaped configuration surrounds a courtyard made common to all dormitories with its stair entries and brick-patterned walkways. Over time, the courtyard has become a popular gathering place for students.

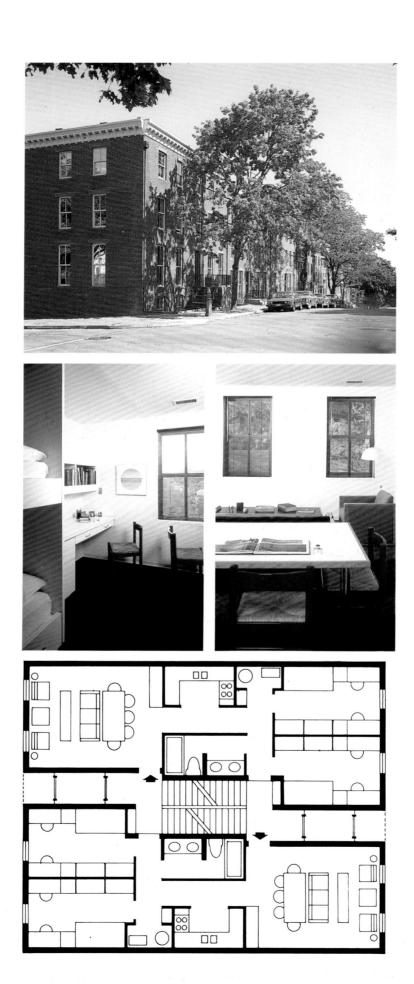

# Karpidas House

*Athens, Greece*

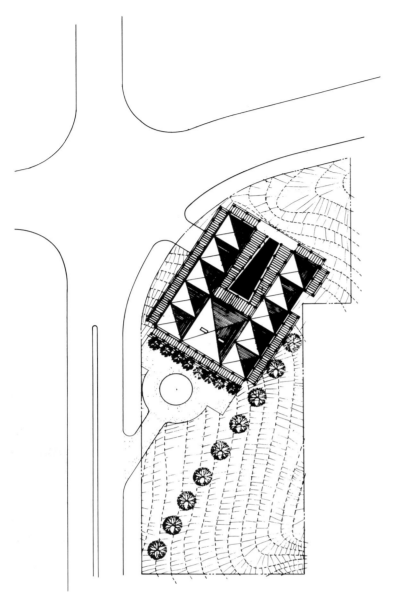

The view from this steep site overlooking the Plain of Attica is surprisingly urban. Athens has grown in all directions, reaching up the slopes that originally defined it. At night, the city's lights fill this ancient and historic basin with a beauty previously unknown. Rather undistinguished suburban villas surround the site and tend to diminish the unique and rare value of the view. For these reasons, this house takes advantage of a downhill gap between two of the neighboring villas, and projects its major axis between them.

The U-shaped plan directs attention to the view in the major rooms. The house is surrounded by sunscreens whose tall supporting columns form an atrium along the major axis; the house consists of 11 white pyramid-roofed pavilions, floored in dark green marble with white veining, and united by the continuous colonnade of sunscreens. The composition rests on a podium that follows the steep grade, with the living floor of the house at entry level. The Acropolis-like podium places the house high above its street approach and offers the promise of something special within. Seven of the major rooms look across the atrium pool to the view.

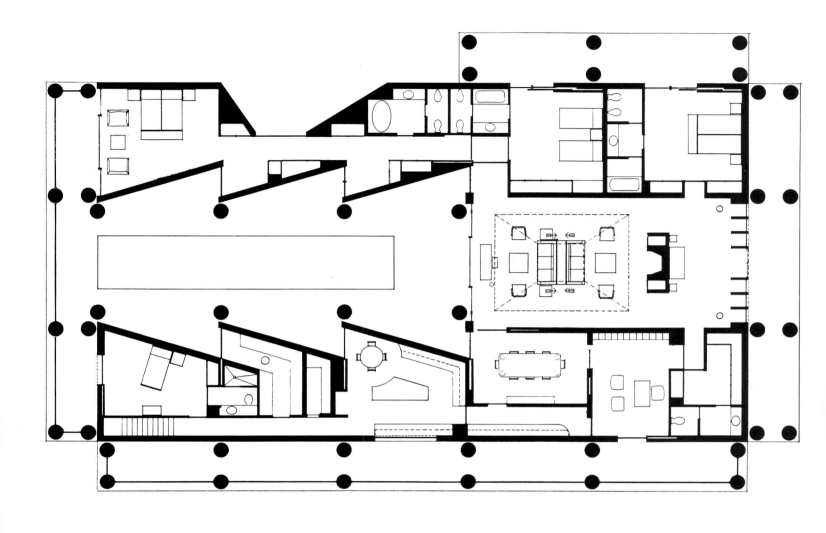

# Welles House

*Bowling Green, Ohio*

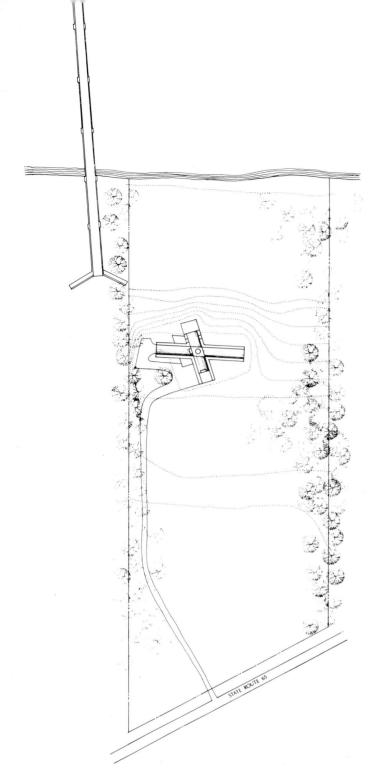

There is a reciprocity between this house and the nearby ruins of an abandoned trolley bridge: The vault of the house echoes the arch of the bridge, which can be seen from every room. Erected in 1904 as part of the interurban rail system connecting Lima and Toledo, the bridge was the largest reinforced-concrete structure in the United States at that time. Today, trees and vines romantically grow from its widening structural faults in a manner that would have pleased Piranesi.

The house has a modified cruciform plan. The longitudinal axis parallels the Maumee River; the cross axis is canted 30 degrees, to point toward the bridge. Each interior, as can be seen in the plan, recalls this concept.

Skylights wash the perimeter walls. One 10-foot-diameter bubble at the center of the plan forms a light-filled atrium. The interior is painted white, for the most part, and the floors are Roman travertine. In harmony with the classical overtones of the ruined bridge, the living room furniture reflects the palette of Etruscan frescoes—terra-cotta and faded blue.

STATE ROUTE 65

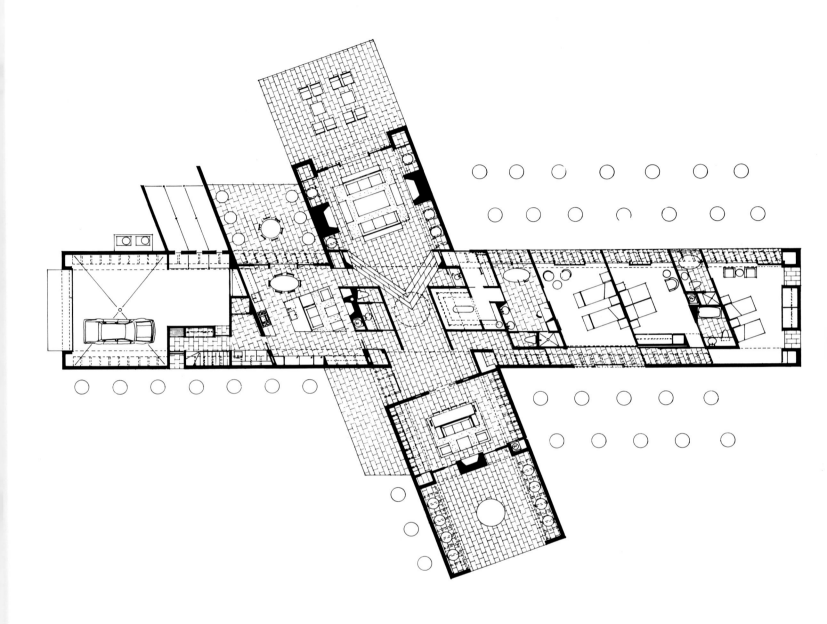

Opposite. View across the
Maumee River, looking south.

Above. Back exterior, looking
northeast.

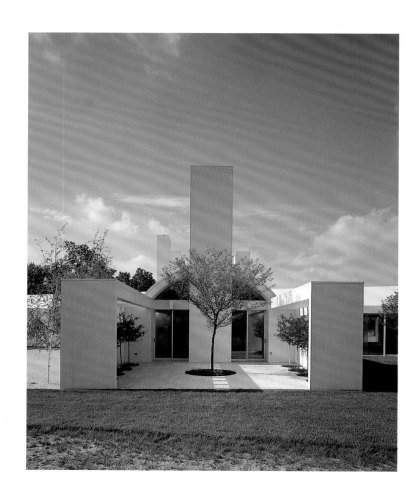

Opposite. Living room interior, looking north.

Above. The interior of the library/dining room.

Above. The northeast outdoor
dining area.

Opposite. The master bedroom
with sliding glass doors.

# Hotel Talleyrand

*Paris, France*

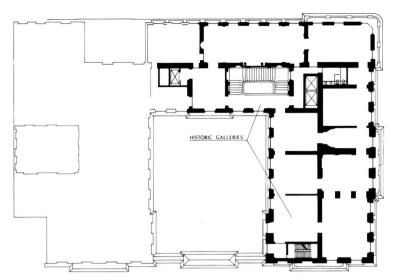

HISTORIC GALLERIES

Restoration of the 18th-century Hotel Talleyrand began in 1980. The aim of the renovation was to provide efficient, modern, flexible office and gallery spaces while retaining the historic fabric of the structure. The final design met the building's program requirements, preserving 6,000 square feet for museum and exhibit space and maintaining relative invisibility for the 20th-century infrastructure essential to the building's modern use.

Since seven of the Hotel Talleyrand's eight facades are under the control of the Historic Monuments Commission of the city of Paris, any exterior modification had to be approved. Interior renovation required a review by the U.S. Department of State's Office of Foreign Buildings.

A monument to 18th-century French architecture, the Hotel Talleyrand overlooks the Place de la Concorde and was built in 1767 after a design by Ange-Jacques Gabriel, architect to Louis XV. The interiors were designed by Jean-Francois Chalgrin. The building was the principal residence of Charles Maurice de Talleyrand, famous for his role in late-18th- and early-19th-century French politics, primarily the rise and fall of Napoleon. From Talleyrand's death in 1838 until renovation began in 1980, this 60,000-square-foot *hotel particulaire* endured many dramatic changes, incursions, and defilements, variously serving as a Belle Epoch residence, as a World War I hospital, as a German naval office during the Second World War, and as headquarters for the U.S. Marshall Plan in the 1950s. It now serves as an important part of the United States Embassy in Paris.

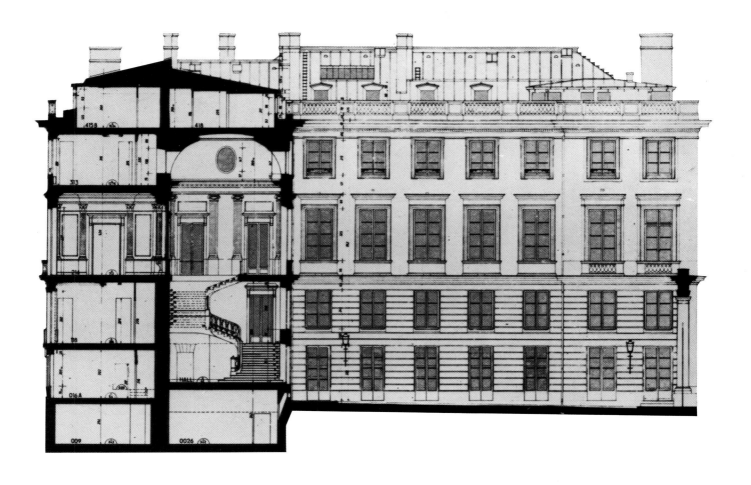

Opposite. The restored grand-stair hall.

Above. The grand-stair hall's ceiling.

Top and bottom left. Before restoration.

Top right. Detail of restored woodwork.
Bottom right. A restored Empire mantelpiece flanked by boiserie from the Pavilion Du Barry Louveciennes by the great architect Ledoux.

Above. The Salon de l'Aigle,
overlooking the Place de la
Concorde.

# Rosenak House

*Tesuque, New Mexico*

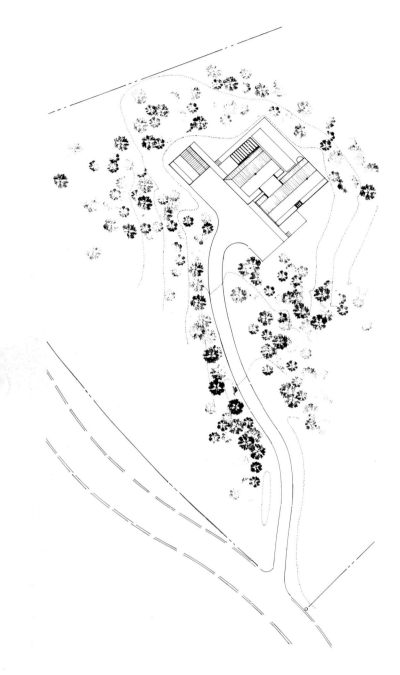

The arid, piñon-dotted land west of Santa Fe is part of an immense desert landscape. Sixteen miles from the nearest town, this polychromed gathering of three simple western buildings is sited between two enormous panoramas: Mountain peaks and forests lie behind it, and the great valley of the Rio Grande lies before it.

The residence was largely designed to display the owner's collection of more than 4,000 pieces of North American folk art. The environs recall the unexploited American West of a century ago. The lighthearted treatment of the facade reflects both a nostalgia for that era and the owner's own appreciation for the ingenuity, independence, and eccentricity of American folk art. In this spirit, shadows are painted permanently in place on the faces of the "frontier town" storefronts.

The buildings are situated so that the "barn" deliberately conceals the vast panorama to the west until that view is framed by a wall of glass in the living room. The house presents two distinct and separate facades on arrival, revealing itself as a single building only after the visitor enters.

The interiors are designed to display art and take advantage of the dramatic views. The terrace and the floors throughout the house are surfaced in local brick. A boardwalk forms the perimeter, erasing the borders of the interior spaces and extending them visually. The living room and bedroom are fitted with traditional Indian fireplaces. The freestanding "barn" houses the registry and stacks for the owner's growing collection of folk art.

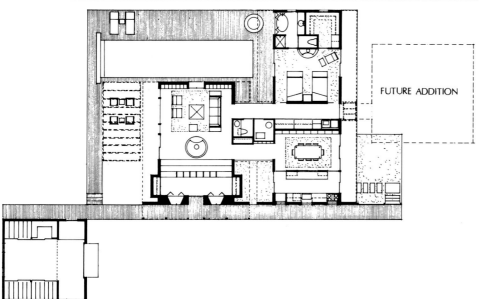

FUTURE ADDITION

Top left. The lap pool.
Bottom left. The disguised barn
conceals pieces of art not on
display in the house.

Top right. The front entry at
night, showing the painted
shadows.
Bottom right. The kitchen
window; the lower shutters are
fixed to conceal the outside wall
and the refrigerator within. The
shadow aligns with nature
around 5:30 on April 23rd.

Top left. The kiva fireplace in
the living room is a traditional
American Indian design, with a
chrome stovepipe.
Bottom left. The master
bedroom and its kiva fireplace.

Top right. An interior view
through the display windows
which flank the entry.
Bottom right. A menagerie of
folk art beasts in the link
between the two buildings.

# Kahn House

*Lima, Ohio*

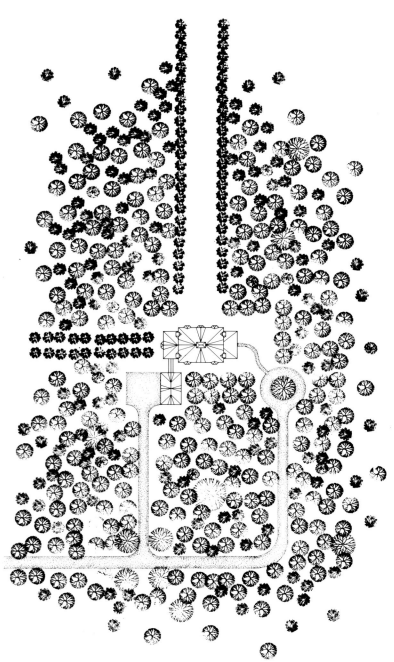

The Ohio of the 19th century was the agricultural heartland of the nation. Today's Ohio is still considered heartland—although it is now perhaps more industrial than agricultural—and visible still, among the interstate highways and the chimneyless factories of modern technology, is the rare, white, board-and-batten, Gothic Revival farmhouse of the past.

The site of this house, not surprisingly, was an abandoned farm. The design of the house reflects the program set out by the clients, a busy obstetrician and his growing family. It consciously abstracts elements from older houses nearby—houses that not only reflect stylistic traditions but also come to terms with the climatic extremes of the region.

The plywood-and-batten house recalls these older farmhouses while minimalizing the details and adding such products of 20th-century technology as insulating glass and thermal, reflective insulation to the 19th-century balloon-frame exterior. A factory-coated metal roof whose battens align with those on the walls of the house contributes to the desired verticality of the design and continues the implied architectural order.

The center-hall plan, attached burgundy "barn," and oversized glass cupola also borrow from historical architectural forms. The "barn" is connected to the house by a glass-enclosed link, veiled with trellis screens; it contains a guest suite above the four-stall garage. Eleven bay windows focus views from the interior of the house on the woodland. A long allée cut through the scrub on axis with the living room's bay windows heightens the sense of domain.

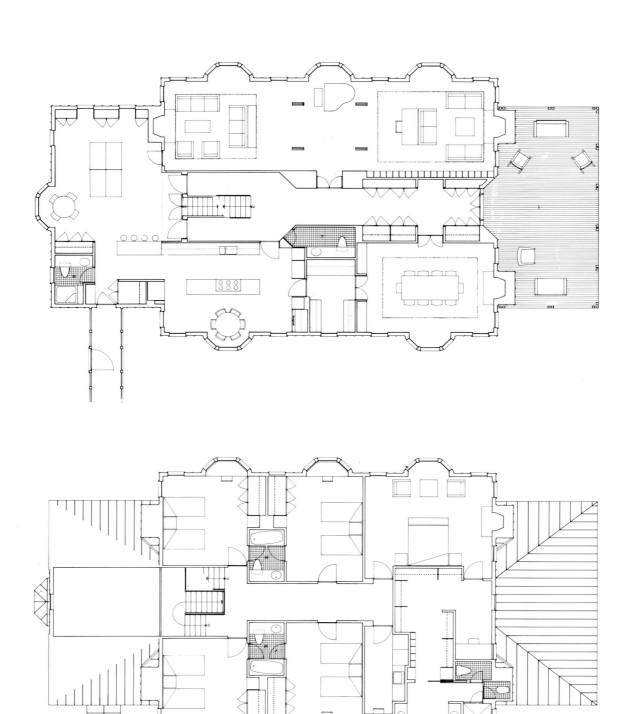

Winter and summer views of the
house at twilight, from the allée.

Top. The library and a wall of eggcrate bookshelves.

Bottom. Looking through the music room, from the library, into the living room.

Top. The breakfast bay in the kitchen.
Bottom left. The breakfast room bay and breezeway.

Bottom right. The kitchen and the service island.
Opposite. An axial view of the dining room, with pantry and kitchen, beyond.

# Voorhees House

*Nantucket, Massachusetts*

Since 1757, seven generations of Nantucket families have had their ways with this particular house. Alterations, both inside and out, have been made with equal measures of irresponsibility and disrespect. For its new owner, the house was peeled like an onion of all intrusions added after 1757. What remained were two stories and a garret clad in weathered shingles and white trim. In addition to two stairways and some odd little service spaces, the interior comprised three rooms on each floor.

Without adding partitions but by removing one (with the help of some steel), the functions of these spaces were once again reshuffled to meet current needs. The front parlor became a new dining room. The odd service space at the rear was combined with the 18th-century kitchen and laundry to make a new living room at the back of the house, where the old kitchen garden would serve as a peaceful prospect. The new kitchen was assigned to the space remaining between front and back. Bathrooms were fitted easily into the existing series of small service spaces on each level.

The floors and wood trim of the interior were patiently stripped by the owner to reveal 200-year-old polychrome trim, untouched and beautifully patinated. Three of the original partitions were faced with painted wood paneling to conceal connecting doors. This abstraction of early New England wood paneling created compartments that conceal a television, a bar, closets, staircases, and the connecting doors. The result is a series of simple spaces that evoke the spirit of the 18th century and essence of a Nantucket house.

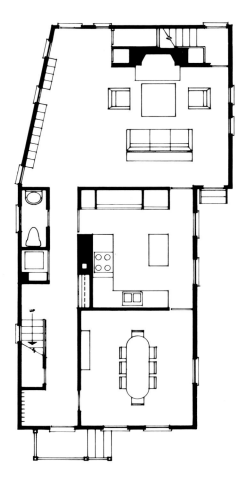

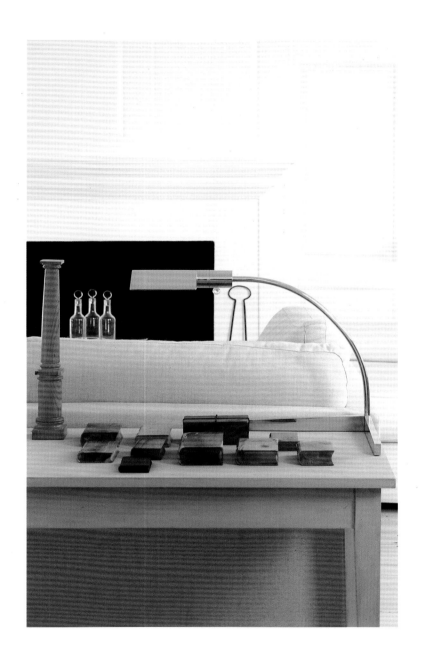

# Bryan House

*Suburban Maryland*

This large residence is located at the crest of a 75-acre site in the rolling horse country of Maryland. The broad scope of the owner's program and the prominent location of the house led to the design of a cluster of nine connecting and sometimes interlocking pavilions. The residence creates the visual impression of an intimate, village-like gathering of farm buildings when it is viewed from a distance or approached from the long entrance drive.

Only a third of the massing can be appreciated from any one perspective. The many parts are unified by the angle of the steeply sloping slate roofs, the rhythm and coloration of the masonry coursing, and the sentinel-like relationship of the boldly vertical chimney masses. Stone flooring passes beneath floor-to-ceiling glass bays and window openings to merge the interior of the house with its exterior terracing; beyond this foreground, one's eye is directed to the distant vistas.

The most important design element in the relationship of the house to its rural surroundings is the living room's axial, outward focus across the fields toward a historic stone church and steeple a quarter of a mile away. As the plan shows, the composition curves backward, away from this paramount visual emphasis, and in so doing creates a central space within the cluster. This is the entry courtyard, reached through a porte cochere from the drive. Principal in this enclosure is a magnificent copper beech, about which the entire design composition revolves. Daniel Urban Kiley designed the landscape in sympathy with the implied order of the house.

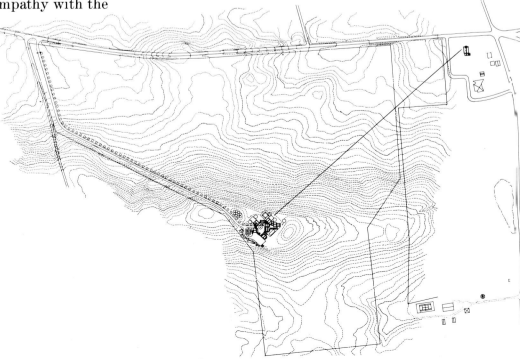

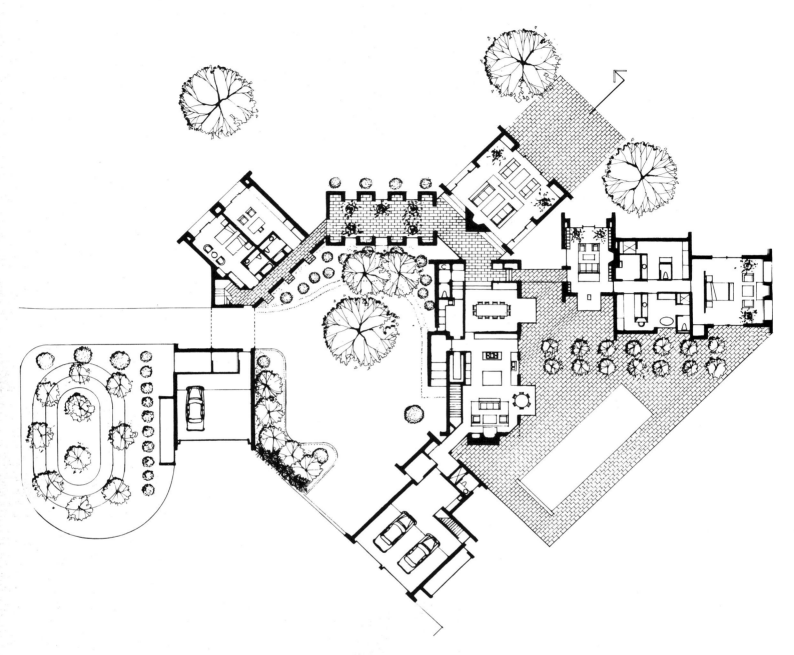

Top. The twelve pavilions are
scattered in a seemingly
innocent pattern, but when seen
from within, they are united by
the major and minor axes of
each module and its links.

Opposite. The design of the
entry pavilion on the right was
based on 18th-century "lantern"
houses, buildings whose windows
align on opposite elevations, thus
giving the appearance of being
lit from within.

274

# Mendoza House

*La Romana, Dominican Republic*

The south coast of the island of Hispaniola is astonishingly straight as it stretches due east from Santo Domingo, the Dominican Republic's capital city. The shoreline is formed by the distinctly nonheroic, seemingly endless cliffs of coral that give it its remarkably linear and deliberate edge.

This house is sited on the edge of the cliffs, overlooking a grove of coconut palms growing out of the delta formed by one of the many clear, freshwater rivers that flow into the Caribbean Sea.

Reflecting the scale and forms of the houses in the nearby fishing village of Bahibe, the corridor-free, seven-pavilion house looks out at the ever-changing light of the sea across a swimming pool, its view defined by the formal podium on which it rests. All but one of its major rooms share this view, and some spaces enjoy three and even four exposures.

The furniture, lighting devices, and weather vane were all specifically designed and fabricated in the Dominican Republic for the island home. The floors— indeed, the entire podium—is surfaced with a white, travertine-like marble quarried on the island. The seven buildings and the screen walls are made of stucco applied over the local cinder block, which is capable of resisting the hurricanes that periodically hover about in early autumn. The roofs are made of imported cedar shingles applied over expressed purlins. An eighth pavilion serves as an entry. Roofless, its exposed rafters were designed to filter the Caribbean sun.

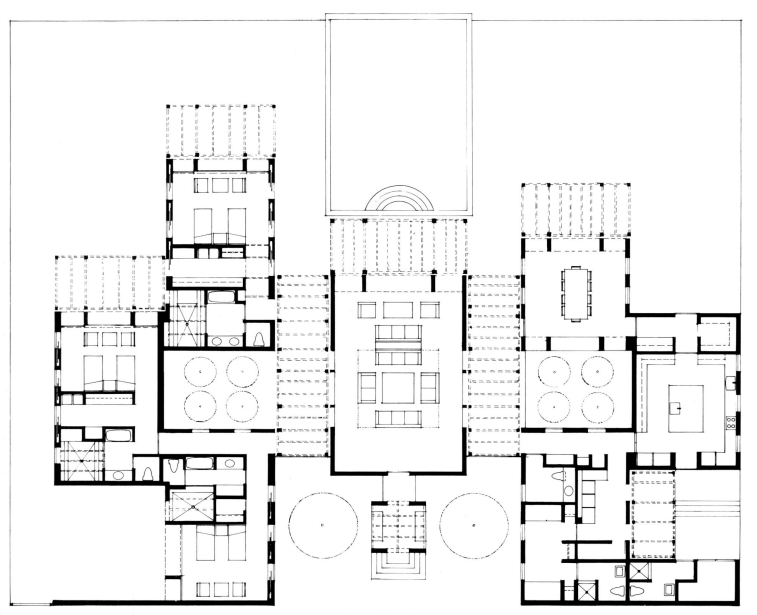

Top. The plan reflects the
relative simplicity in climates
that are friendly to the human
species. This climate eliminates
glazing, insect screens, weather
stripping, thresholds, heating,
insulation, and corridors.
Opposite. One of two
sunscreened passages on the
right joins the living-room
pavilion with the others in the
gathering.

Opposite. The living room as seen from the entry door. All of the furniture and lamps were designed by the architect and fabricated in the Dominican Republic.

Above. The dining pavilion, looking toward one of a pair of interior courtyards.

# Advaney House

*The Netherlands*

This house is sited on the edge of a small private lake that is surrounded by a rare forest of black oak trees, once part of a 19th-century estate.

The building recalls 15th- and 16th-century Dutch houses; made from the same small brick, it is painted white and composed of eight stepped gables. The windows are divided into squares on the gable ends and are clear glass on the eave sides, allowing the interior spaces to frame the water and forest views.

The house is entered through a small gable, where the major axis opens onto a tree-lined and skylit interior "street" that serves every room within. The house will be completed in 1989.

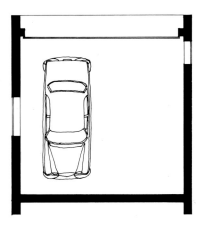

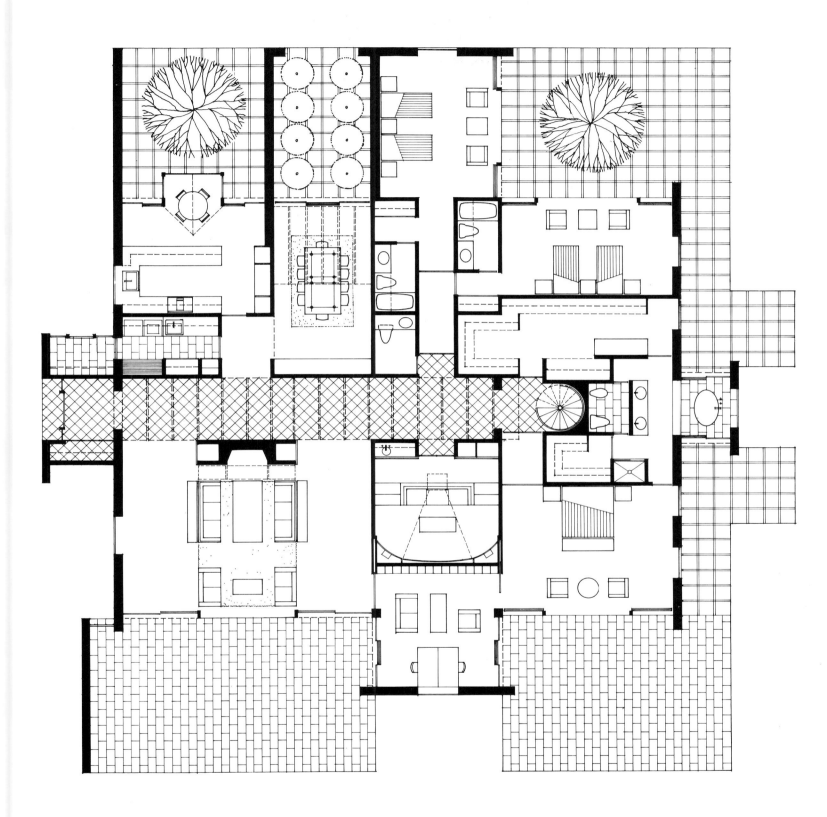

# Jacobs House

*Meadowbrook, Pennsylvania*

This house's entry drive leaves the street almost furtively as it penetrates a dense evergreen hedge of white pine and hemlock. The drive slopes gently down a deeply wooded hillside away from the street. Then, appropriately, it makes one turn that nearly reverses the original direction. The house and garage are aligned parallel with the slope of the hill and separated by the 25-foot-wide "street" that is defined by them.

The form of the house comprises five distinct shapes that recall the profiles, articulation, and massing of the domestic architecture of the region. The chimneys are exaggerated in height, and the roof shapes play off one another, aligned as they are on seemingly separate pavilions made more distinct by the different materials of their construction. The roofs of all five pavilions are cedar shingle, while the wood siding and brick of the pavilions are painted white, to contrast with the deep green forest surrounding the house.

The upper-level interior spaces of the house address the entry "street" and express the advantages of the delineated pavilions and roof forms. The two-story living room reaches for the light entering the six dormer windows that accent its roof. The entry receives natural light through openings on both facades, like an 18th-century lantern house. The library, on the lower level, is open to the space above and shares the light from one quarter of the pavilion-defining pyramidal roof some 25 feet above.

All of the lower-level bedrooms are 10 feet in height and open through sliding pocket-doors onto stone terraces and soft green lawns that are defined by the tall, dark edge of the woodland. Twenty-foot-wide allées cut through the wood to create two tall, defined avenues of light that lead the eye down the unexpectedly long slope to the open meadows below and the distant blue hills beyond. The house is scheduled for completion in 1988.

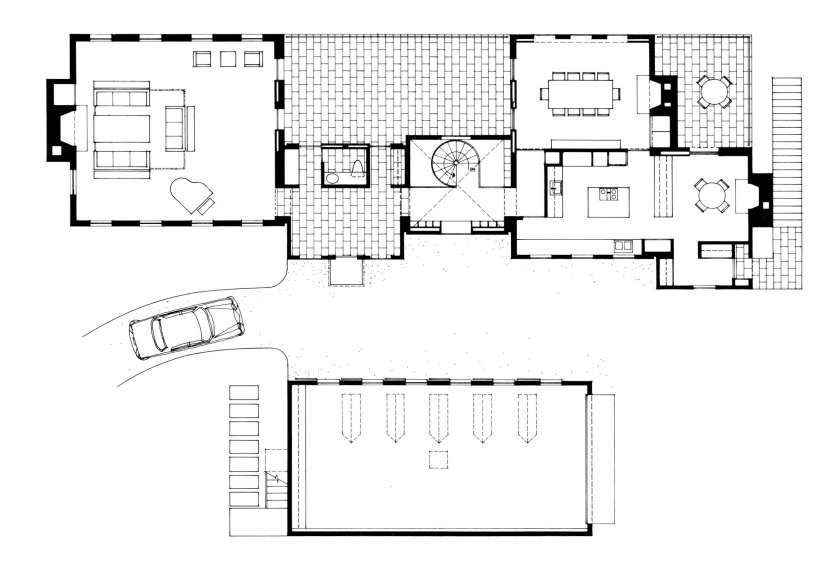

# Forbes House

*Bloomfield Hills, Michigan*

This balanced house of neoclassical proportions is sited to take maximum advantage of views over not one but two lakes.

The square serves as the order of proportion here, in both plan and elevation. From the smallest window panes to the proportions of the openings and the dimensions of the walls, the rhythms and relationships of the square prevail.

The approach along a public street deliberately leads one nearly past the house before the entry drive is announced. An opening in a grove of trees exposes the entrance pavilion at the end of an ordered allée of pear trees. The subsequent progression of spatial experiences—approaching the house, entering the first pavilion, proceeding along the same axis until the effect of the space and light of the great room is realized—is, it is hoped, worthy of the final view across the small island and the lake beyond.

The four-part house is faced with a salmon-colored brick and banded with buff limestone coursing. The pale green slate roof forms are lightly delineated in oxidized copper, and the slate terraces are a pale green as well. The house is scheduled for completion in 1988.

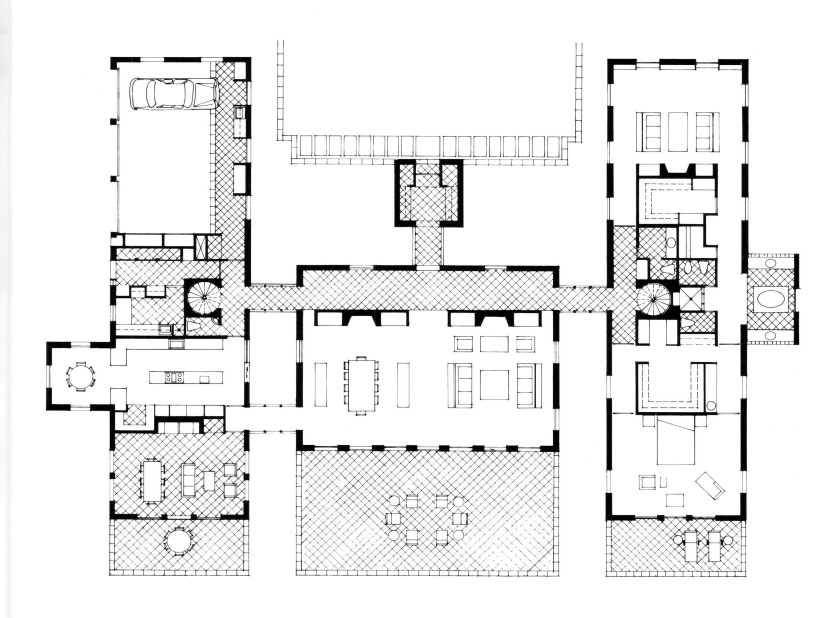

297

# Carson House

*Dutchess County, New York*

The approach to this house is an ascent. The row of
trees that initially parallels its private drive is soon
reinforced with a formal double-row of maples that
point up the slope to a lone, windowless pavilion whose
single peak is silhouetted against the sky. The house is
actually first revealed through a parting of the tree
rows on the left. The drive then drops to a gravel
entrance court embraced by four seemingly separate
pavilions surrounding a large, umbrella-like tree.

The pavilions—there are five altogether—are topped
with pyramidal roofs of cedar shingle; the pavilion
sited on axis with the entrance court has a tall, white,
painted brick chimney at its center. The seeming
separateness of the pavilions helps to reduce the
apparent mass of this house upon a hill. Each of the
pavilions serves a different function: master bedroom,
entry/living room, dining room/kitchen (with children's
bedrooms above), guest house, and garage. Three of the
pavilions are connected by glass links that are nearly
invisible when viewed from the entry court.

The pavilions are clad in board-and-batten, and it is
intended that each be painted in a different color
drawn from the surrounding 18th-century farmhouses:
burgundy, white, dark green, barn red, and black,
respectively. This color palette, together with the
decision to site the house a bit below the peak of the
hill, allows the tall white chimney alone to announce
its domain. One hopes that the color and forms of the
architectural gathering below will enhance, rather than
intrude upon, the natural appearance of the hill. The
house is scheduled for completion in 1988.

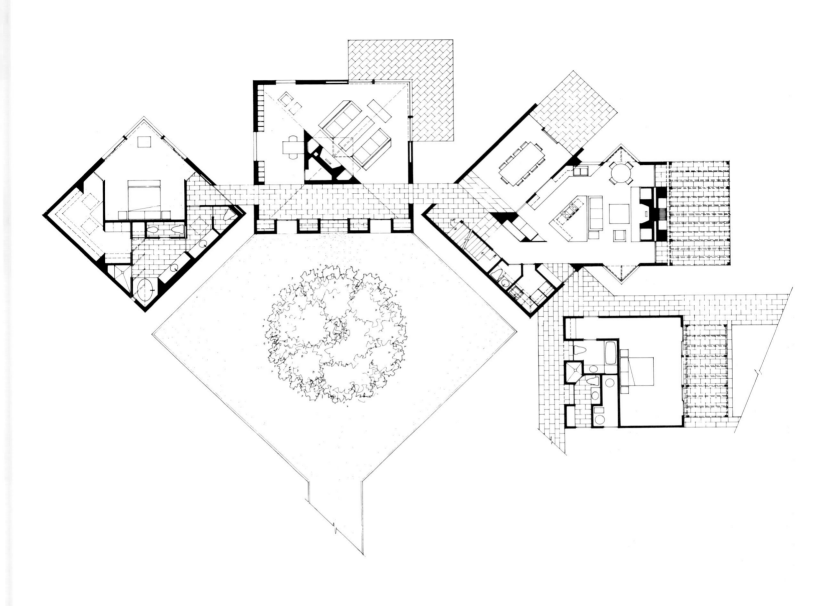

# Waddell House

*Long Island, New York*

This house is sited to withhold the long view. Its approach road winds through bayberry and pine— particularly tantalizing after a three-hour drive from the city. Suddenly, the sandy road straightens and aligns itself dramatically with the all-glass entry that connects the major two of this house's five pyramid-roofed structures, gathered to form a highly ordered forecourt. Four tall chimneys announce the important pavilion and establish a sense of place, and a spectacular view is promised as the sea's horizon is glimpsed through the glazed entry that is the only opening in the walled forecourt.

The house and its respective outbuildings are placed upon a white brick podium that seems to grow out of the slope, and that respects the tall cliff which falls sharply to the Atlantic below. In the living room, a large bay window affords the long view down the coast and out to the ever-changing light of the sea.

At the center of the house, the four chimneys enclose a skylit stair that ascends to the master suite above. From the exterior, it is hoped, these tall chimneys will visually reinforce the height of the cliff when seen from the sea. The brick walls of the house are painted white, and all of the roofs and terraces are a gray-green stone from England. The kitchen garden is walled, to protect it from both the Atlantic winds and the elegantly distracting deer that live in the surrounding gorse. The house is scheduled for completion in late 1988.

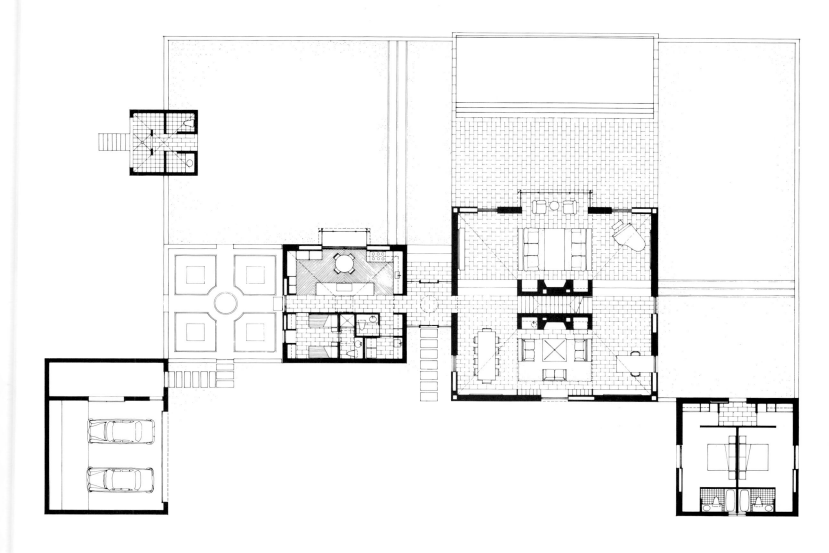

# Glossary

# Glossary

The eloquence in the language of architecture is measured by how a building is put together. The joining of materials in a manner that retains the integrity of each part, while assigning a function compatible and advantageous to its nature, has always been a measure of "seriousness" in architecture.

"God is in the details"—a phrase attributed to Mies and revered by all of us as we endeavor again and again to do the right thing. Architecture is order, and this order carries throughout the building down to the smallest corner. There is no back side to architecture any more than there is a detail that is unimportant. Detailing expresses the "how" of buildings and when done with great care and skill reinforces the "why." It can express the honesty not only of the architecture but of all those involved in the making of it. It is a slow process whose results are seldom noticed. It has been said that good detailing should never show the agony it took to produce it, but should appear as if it had not been detailed at all, as if it went together the way it wanted to go together—or as Lou Kahn has said, "the way it wants to be."

The details illustrated on the next six pages form a glossary as they are the language of the buildings herein. They are details that occur repeatedly in this book, not because they are a solution, but because they approached a solution to a certain problem that kept reoccurring in different buildings. Many of the details that follow address a one-of-a-kind problem and cannot be applied again—nor should they. It is fair to say that very few would "work" together in a single building, because each detail belongs to a family that is inherent with the building for which it was created.

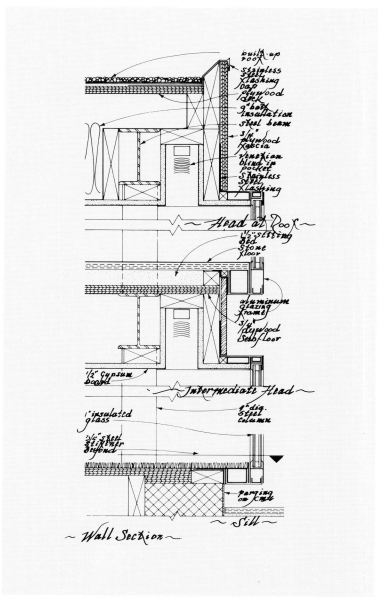

~ Wall Section ~

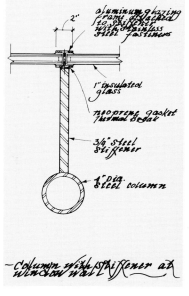

~ Column with Stiffener at Window Wall ~

Fascia with continuous vent slot.

Wall with concealed gutter and vent slot.

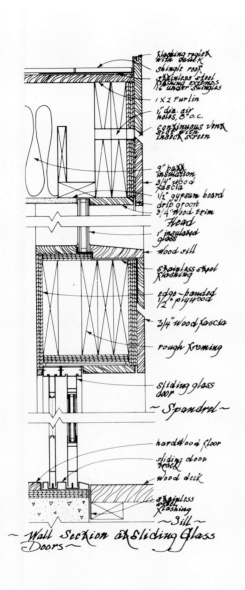

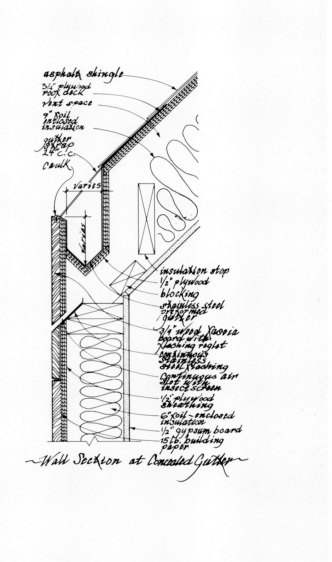

Wall Section at Sliding Glass Doors

~Wall Section at Concealed Gutter~

Axonometric sectional detail of
house wall.

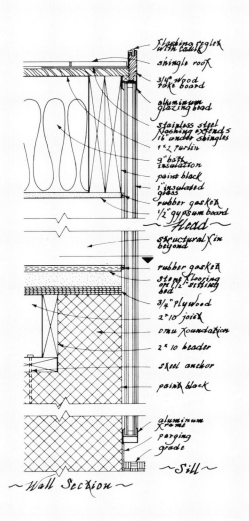

Top. Skylight.
Bottom. Curtain-wall structural
fins.

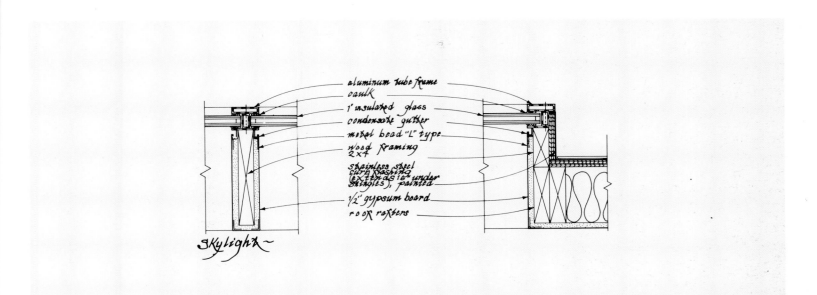

aluminum tube frame
caulk
1' insulated glass
condensate gutter
metal bead "L" type
wood framing
2×4
stainless steel
curb flashing
(extends under
shingles), painted
1/2" gypsum board
roof rafters

*Skylight~*

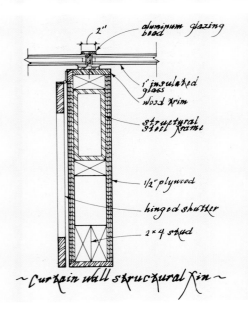

2"
aluminum glazing
bead
1' insulated
glass
wood trim
structural
steel frame
1/2" plywood
hinged shutter
2×4 stud

*~Curtain wall structural fin~*

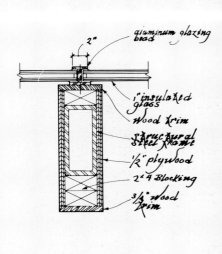

2"
aluminum glazing
bead
1' insulated
glass
wood trim
structural
steel frame
1/2" plywood
2×4 blocking
3/4" wood
trim

*~Curtain wall structural fin~*

Below. The gable end with its
ridge vent.

Top right. Ceiling ridge with
open seam.
Bottom right. Concealed pocket
door head.

Above. The pocket door as
seen from the living room.

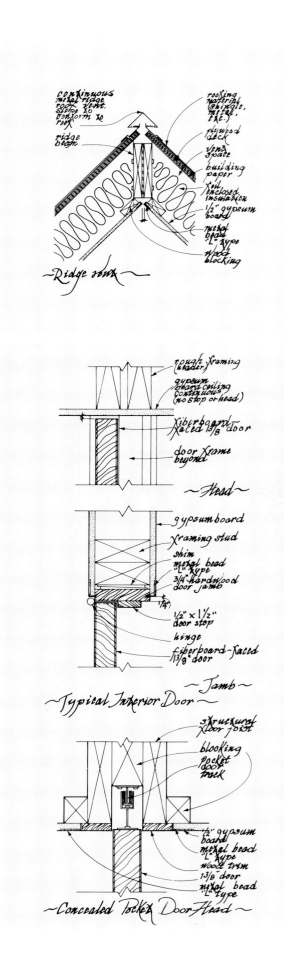

Below. Wood grille for return air, in the hall.

Top right. Return-air grille. Bottom right. Eggcrate bookcase.

Above. The eggcrate bookshelves.

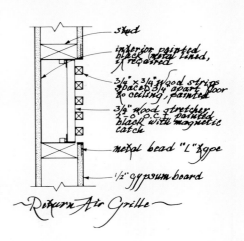

~Return Air Grille~

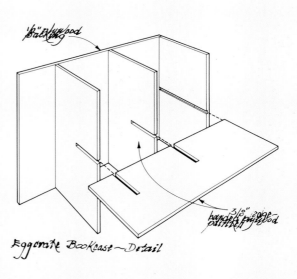

Eggcrate Bookcase~Detail

# Chronology

**1958**

**Roberts House**
West Virginia, 1958

**1959**

**Thoron House**
Suburban Maryland, 1959

**Branscomb House**
Holly Hill, Maryland, 1959

**1960**

**Tager House**
Bethesda, Maryland, 1960
*Landscape architect: Lester Collins, FASLA*

**Nathan House**
Bethesda, Maryland, 1960
Addition 1987

**1961**

**A Victorian House Remodeled**
Washington, D.C., 1961
*Landscape architect: Lester Collins, FASLA*

**1962**

**Carter House**
Washington, D.C., 1962
Addition 1967

318

This simple house, built almost entirely of California redwood, was neither plumbed nor wired. Post and beam defined the frame; planked deck and roof structure stated the purpose. Half of the building's tongue-and-groove skin was formed of panels that slid laterally to open an equal percentage of the interior to the elements. A great chimney mass anchored this basic structure to the side of its West Virginia mountain.

The house, with its view across the narrows of the Potomac River far below, was totally destroyed by fire a few short years after the carload of its timber arrived from California. The heat of the forest fire was so intense that the house exploded, totally erasing the stone chimney and all other evidence of this first effort. Nothing remains.

See page 12.

The site of this brick hillside house is adjacent to that of the Thoron House. The plan reflects the response of the design to the definite program demands of the young clients. In the spirit of the time, the house is fitted with a complete underground fallout shelter.

This large rectangular box of a house has bedrooms and living areas on the entry level with playroom, staff, and storage areas on the lower level. Designed with the owner's four children in mind, the house has a special kids' entrance with a washable concrete floor. Most of the rooms open onto landscaped patios. The property is surrounded by woods.

Award for Excellence in Architecture, Masonry Institute, 1961

*Washington Star,* Dec. 10, 1960

A cruciform plan isolating the garage with a portecochere took advantage of a gorge running through the site; the house has many levels, and all of the rooms except one have access to the exterior at grade. The entry, with its large bubble skylight over the stair, disarmingly explains the plan.

*Washington Star,* Oct. 1, 1965

The mass and facade of an identical row house were added to the original building here, with the two linked by an entry way. The front of the house maintains a Victorian character, complying with the Old Georgetown Act, while the back satisfies the architectural orders of the current day.

Award for Excellence in Architecture, Potomac Valley Chapter/AIA, 1962
Award of Merit, New York Chapter/ AIA, 1964

*Design Action,* Sept. 10, 1982: 2
*House Beautiful,* Sept. 1963: 154–157
National Trust For Historic Preservation *Old and New Architecture Design Relationships* (1980): 110
*New York Herald Tribune,* Nov. 10, 1964
*New York Times,* Apr. 19, June 19, 1962; Nov. 8, 1964

O'Brien, G. *The New York Times Book of Interior Design and Decoration* (1965): 162–165
*Progressive Architecture,* Mar. 1964: 158–159
*Washington Post Magazine,* Sept. 25, 1977: 30
*Washington Star,* June 23, July 2, 1962

Originally completed in 1907, this pebbledash-stuccoed, all-American house was nearly totally redesigned twice for its second owners. The first renovation in 1962 reassigned the interior spaces and relocated the front entry. A podium was created to raise the grade to the level of the first floor.

A large playroom and outdoor loggia with swimming pool were added five years later, allowing the house to respond to the changing lives of the active family.

*House & Garden,* May 1963: 144

**Shorb House**
Bethesda, Maryland, 1962

**Vest Guest House**
Washington, D.C., 1962

**1963**

**Naftalin House**
Riva, Maryland, 1963

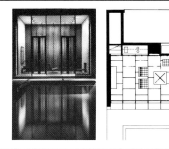

**Beech House**
West Tisbury, Massachusetts, 1963

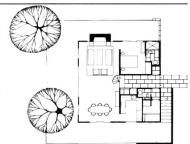

**Oliver House**
McLean, Virginia, 1963

**Shaw House**
New York City, 1963

**1965**
*A Guide to the Architecture of Washington, D.C.,* edited by Hugh Newell Jacobsen

**Gainer House**
Suburban Virginia, 1965

320

See page 18.

Award for Excellence in Architecture, Metropolitan Washington Board of Trade, 1962
Award for Excellence in Architecture, *Architectural Record,* 1964

*Architectural Record,* "Houses of 1964," May 1964: 64–67
*Washington Post,* Sept. 11, 1964
*Washington Star,* Oct. 1, 1965

---

This guest house was fitted carefully into the back of a pool-filled garden in Washington's most historic district. A deliberate departure from the Colonial style of the main house, it serves as a focus for views across the tranquil pool. It contains an 18-foot-high main room whose walnut paneling conceals kitchenette, bar, and stairs leading to a bedroom and bath a half-level above.

Award for Excellence in Architecture, Metropolitan Washington Board of Trade, 1965

*House & Garden,* July 1967: 92–93
Metropolitan Washington Board of Trade 23rd Biennial Awards (GH)

---

Award of Merit, New York Chapter/AIA, 1964
First Honor Award, AIA with *American Home* and *House & Home,* Homes for Better Living Program, 1965
Award for Excellence in Achitecture, *Architectural Record,* 1965
Award for Excellence in Architecture and Best in Competition, Potomac Valley Chapter/AIA, 1965

Award of Merit, Baltimore Chapter/AIA and the Chamber of Commerce of Metropolitan Baltimore

*Ameryka,* No. 489: 22–23
*Architect's Report,* Fall 1965 (Chesapeake Bay Region)
*Architectural Record,* May 1965; Feb. 1966
*Aujourd'hui,* Jan. 1967: 28–29
Harling, R. *House & Garden Guide to*

*Interior Decoration* (1967): 52
*House & Garden,* May 1965: 130–133
*House & Garden Building Guide,* Spring 1968
*House & Garden Guide for Young Living,* Spring 1968
*House & Home,* June 1965: 74–75
*House Beautiful Building Manual,* Spring 1968
*New York Times,* Nov. 8, Nov. 22, 1964

O'Brien, G. *The New York Times Book of Interior Design and Decoration* (1965): 170–171
*Potomac Valley Architect,* 5th Biennial Competition, Dec. 1964
Smith, H. L. *The Architectural Record Book of Vacation Houses* (1970): 150
*Tochi–Jutaku,* Nov. 1968: 41–47
*Washington Post,* Nov. 10, Dec. 5, 1965
*Washington Star,* Dec. 4, 1964

---

See page 20.

Honorable Mention, AIA with *American Home* and *House & Home,* Homes for Better Living Program, 1966
Award for Excellence in Architecture, *Architectural Record,* 1966

*Architectural Record,* May 1966: 47–49
*Boston Magazine,* "Who Owns the Vineyard?" Aug. 1980: 102–112
*House & Home,* July 1966
*House Beautiful,* June 1965: 120
Smith, H. L. *The Architectural Record Book of Vacation Houses* (1970): 188

---

This gazebo in the garden was designed to serve as an object to be viewed year-round from the nearly all-glass living room of the main house, whose main axis crosses that of the garden structure. Serving as a summer dining pavilion, it is fitted with floor-to-ceiling screens, stone floors, and an elaborate grill for outdoor cooking. It is built of cypress.

*Washington Post Potomac Magazine,* Aug. 4, 1968

---

The renovation of this 1880s brownstone on New York City's Upper West Side partially returned this building to its original use. A two-story living room was carved out within, and took advantage of the previously overlooked potential of the city garden at the rear of the house.

Award of Merit, New York Chapter/AIA, 1967

*Architectural Record,* Mar. 1966: 158
*Architecture and Urbanism,* Nov. 1973: 140
Hatje and Kaspar *1601 Decorating Ideas for Modern Living* (1974): 77
*House Beautiful Home Remodeling,* Fall 1967: cover, 128–131
*Interiors,* Feb. 1966: 96–97
*New York Times,* Mar. 1967

---

This house, clad in tongue-and-groove cypress and surrounded by a wooden deck, appears one story tall when approached. The central cylinder, which contains a spiral stair, continues through the roof plane. The upper level is an open plan with four finite zones: entry, living, dining, and kitchen.

An oak-stripped "box"—not touching the ceiling—allows the plan to remain open while defining the kitchen zone. The memory overlay of Johnson's glass house is reasonably evident here.

Award for Excellence in Architecture, Metropolitan Washington Board of Trade, 1966
Honorable Mention, AIA with *American*

*Home* and *House & Home,* Homes for Better Living Program, 1968
Award for Excellence in Architecture, Northern Virginia Chapter/AIA, 1969

*Architectural Record,* Feb. 1968: 78–81
*Home/Life,* Sept. 12, 1976: 44
*House & Home,* July 1968: 95
*House Beautiful,* July 1967: 88–91
*House Beautiful Building Manual,* Fall/

Winter 1968–69: 128–131
Metropolitan Washington Board of Trade 24th Biennial Awards, 1967
Smith, H. L. *The Architectural Record Book of Vacation Houses* (1970): 86–90
Wagner, W. F. Jr., FAIA, ed. *Great Houses* (1976): 175–177
*Washington Post,* May 31, 1969
*Washington Post Potomac Magazine,* Sept. 17, Oct. 29, 1967; Mar. 16, 1969

**Cafritz House**
Georgetown, Washington, D.C., 1965

**Jacobsen House**
2735 P Street, N.W.
Georgetown, Washington, D.C., 1960
and 1965

**1966**

**A Brick Pavilioned House**
Washington, D.C., 1966

**Scott House**
Georgetown, Washington, D.C.,
1966 and 1972

**1967**

**Bolton Square**
Baltimore, Maryland, 1967

**Millett House**
Bristol, Rhode Island, 1967

**1968**

**Hartman Addition**
Northwest Washington, D.C., 1968

322

See page 24.

Award for Excellence in Architecture, Potomac Valley Chapter/AIA, 1966
Award for Excellence in Architecture, Metropolitan Washington Board of Trade, 1966

*Architecture and Urbanism,* Nov. 1973: 168
National Trust For Historic Preservation *Old and New Architecture Design Relationships* (1980): 111
*Home Furnishings Daily,* Oct. 11, 1966
*Life,* Nov. 4, 1966: 98–103
Metropolitan Washington Board of Trade 24th Biennial Awards, 1967
Von Eckardt, W. *A Place to Live* (1967): 236–237

*Washington Star,* Dec. 16, 1966
*Washington Star Sunday Magazine,* June 4, 1967

---

The architect practiced out of the basement of this house for nearly five years. The family's home from 1959–1969, the house is 16 feet wide with four high-ceilinged stories and a walled garden; it was twice remodeled in the decade of residence.

Hatje and Kaspar *1601 Decorating Ideas for Modern Living* (1974): 44–47
*Home Furnishings Daily,* June 14, 1965
*House Beautiful,* Feb. 1967: 132–135
*House Beautiful Building Manual,* Fall/Winter 1967/68: 146–149
*Interiors,* May 1965: 101–103
Reif, R. *Living with Books* (1973): 13
*This Week,* Feb. 6, 1966
*Washington Post,* Feb. 18, 1967

*Washington Post Potomac Magazine,* Mar. 16, Mar. 23, 1969
*Washington Star,* Oct. 6, 1963: 32–36
*Washingtonian,* Dec. 1965

---

See page 28.

Award for Excellence in Architecture, Metropolitan Washington Board of Trade, 1966
Award for Excellence in Architecture, *Architectural Record,* 1967
Award of Merit, AIA with *American Home* and *House & Home,* Homes for Better Living Program, 1967

*Architectural Record,* May 1967: 82–85
*Architecture and Urbanism,* Nov. 1973: 63
*Aujourd'hui,* Jan. 1967: 28–29
Hatje and Kaspar *1601 Decorating Ideas for Modern Living* (1974): 75, 160
*House & Home,* July 1967: 70–71
Metropolitan Washington Board of Trade 24th Biennial Awards, 1967
*Tochi-Jutaku,* Nov. 1968: 41–47
*Washington Post,* Mar. 18, 1973: H1

*Washington Post Potomac Magazine,* Sept. 1966: 38–39
*Washingtonian,* July 1966

---

The first of two alterations for different owners joined these two houses and reassigned the living room to the second floor, where it commands charming views of the garden and street below. A decade later, the third-floor facade was infilled with the addition of another bedroom, completing the composition.

*American Home,* May 1967: 84–86
*Baltimore Sun Magazine,* Apr. 8, 1979: 42–44
*Washington Post,* Apr. 1, 1973: H1

---

See page 36.

Award of Merit, Baltimore Chapter/AIA and the Chamber of Commerce of Metropolitan Baltimore, 1965, 1967
Honorable Mention, AIA with *American Home* and *House & Home,* Homes For Better Living Program, 1968

*Architectural Record,* Jan. 1968: 154–155; June 1969: 43
*Baltimore Magazine,* Dec. 1967
*Baltimore Sun Magazine,* Oct. 1, 1967; May 25, 1969
*Detail,* No. 5, 1968: 909–910
Equitable Trust Co., Baltimore, Annual Report, 1968
*Fortune,* May 1966: 121
*Forum,* May 1966: 57

*Historic Preservation,* Apr. 1968: 55
*House Beautiful,* Aug. 1968: 60–63
*House Beautiful Building Manual,* Spring 1969: 198–201
*House & Garden,* Feb. 1967: 145
*Maryland Living,* Nov. 12, 1967
*Newsfront,* Feb. 1970: 27
*New York Times,* May 25, 1969
*Tochi-Hutaku,* Nov. 1968: 41–47
*Washington Post,* May 25, 1969

---

See page 32.

Award for Excellence in Architecture, *Architectural Record,* 1968
First Honor Award, AIA with *American Home* and *House & Home,* Homes for Better Living Program, 1968

*Architectural Record,* May 1968: 78–81
*Architecture and Urbanism,* Nov. 1973: 63
Faulkner and Ziegfeld *Art Today* (1969): 24–25
Foley, M. M. *The American House* (1980): 271
Hatje and Kaspar *1601 Decorating Ideas for Modern Living* (1974): 75, 160
*House Beautiful,* June 1968: 50–56; May 1969: 142

*House Beautiful Building Manual,* Fall/Winter 1969–70: 114–117
*House & Garden,* Nov. 1975
*House & Home,* Nov. 1968
*Tochi-Hutaku,* Nov. 1968: 41–47

---

This cypress pavilion serves as a breakfast room overlooking a walled-in garden and large pool. It is united with the original house by a comfortable wood deck that runs the length of the garden facade and joins all of the ground-floor rooms with the polite scale of a village street.

*House & Garden,* July–Aug. 1977: 88

**WETA Project**
Washington, D.C., 1968

**1969**
National Honor Award, American Institute of Architects, Bolton Square: *Urban renewal furnished the means for replacing blighted dwellings that formerly occupied the site. Now, Bolton Square has become part of the renaissance of a 19th-century neighborhood near the center of the city.—* Jury comment

**Trentman House**
Washington, D.C., 1969
*Landscape architect: Lester Collins, FASLA*

**Smernoff House**
Bethesda, Maryland, 1969

**Jacobsen House**
Washington, D.C., 1969

**1970**
Visiting professor for the arts and humanities at the American University of Cairo
Member of the president's commission on alumni affairs for Yale University

**Beach House**
Rehoboth Beach, Delaware, 1970

**Tidesfall**
Columbia, Maryland, 1970

**A Bar in Georgetown**
Washington, D.C., 1970

 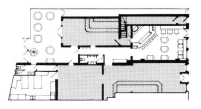

This unrealized project was to have been sited in a highly visible part of Southwest Washington, close to the waterfront, and would have served the dynamic local educational television station.

*Evening Star,* "RLA Expected to Approve WETA Plans," Nov. 18, 1968

---

See page 42.

Award of Merit, Potomac Valley Chapter/AIA, 1968
Award for Excellence in Architecture, Northern Virginia Chapter/AIA, 1969
Award for Excellence in Architecture, *Architectural Record,* 1969
First Honor Award, AIA with *American*

*Home* and *House & Home,* Homes for Better Living Program, 1969
Honor Award, AIA Middle Atlantic Regional Conference, 1969
Award for Excellence in Architecture, Metropolitan Washington Board of Trade, 1969

*Albuquerque Tribune,* Aug. 29, 1979
*Architectural Record,* Apr., May 1969

*Architecture and Urbanism,* Nov. 1973: 170
*Home-Life,* Mar. 18, 1979: 8
*House & Home,* July 1969: 72–73
*House Beautiful,* Apr. 1969: 84–89
*House Beautiful Decorating Manual,* Spring 1970: 150–153
National Trust For Historic Preservation *Old and New Architecture Design Relationships* (1980): 67–68, 147
*New York Times,* Apr. 21, 1969

*Preservation News,* Apr. 1969: 4
*Regardie's,* Apr. 1986: 44–57
Smith, H. L. Jr., AIA *25 Years of Record Houses* (1981): 144–147
Thompson, E. K., FAIA, ed. *Recycling Buildings* (1977): 200–201
*Washington Dossier,* Oct. 1986: 59–64
*Washington Post,* Dec. 14, 1968; July 5, 1969: E3

---

This two-story house on a sloping wooded site is barely visible from the street. Its central pavilion provides orientation—right and left, up and down. Living, dining, and kitchen functions are concentrated in the left pavilion. The right pavilion houses the library as part of the master bedroom suite. The children's bedrooms and staff quarters are on the lower level.

Award for Excellence in Architecture, Metropolitan Washington Board of Trade, 1969
Award for Excellence in Architecture, *Architectural Record,* 1970
Award of Merit, Bethesda-Chevy Chase Chamber of Commerce, 1971

*Architectural Record,* May 1970: 38–41
*Baltimore Sun Magazine,* May 9, 1971: 12–14
*House & Garden Building Guide,* Fall 1972–73: 142–144
*Washington Post,* Apr. 18, 1970 (real estate)
*Washington Star Home Life,* July 3, 1977: 18–21

---

All but two rooms of this two-facade house share a view of the garden. A walled stone terrace and a gentle bank of ivy lead to two rows of American holly, which admit sparkling light through the glass of the garden facade. Three large skylights in the roof help to distribute light within.

*Architectural Digest,* Jan. 1984: 108–113
*Baltimore Sun Magazine,* Mar. 28, 1971
Gilliat, M. *Kitchens and Dining Rooms* (1970): 64–65
*House & Garden,* Mar. 1973: 84–87
*House Beautiful,* Dec. 1977
Maroon, F. J., *Maroon on Georgetown,* 1985: 54–55
Mehlhorn, W. *House & Garden's Book of Remodeling* (1978): 124–127

Mitchell, M. *Glimpses of Georgetown, Past and Present:* 39
Moody, E. *Decorative Art in Modern Interiors* (1973): 46–49
Plumb, B. *Houses Architects Live In* (1977): 128–131
*Town & Country,* Jan. 1985: 142
*Washington Post,* Feb. 18, 1967
*Washington Post Potomac Magazine,* Apr. 13, 1977

*Washington Star,* Apr. 6, 1971; Apr. 7, 1971: B6
*Washington Star Sunday Magazine,* Oct. 30, 1977: 13
*Washingtonian,* Nov. 1976: 114; "Map of the Stars," Aug. 1980: 72; Nov. 1985: 206–207
Wise, H. H. *Attention to Detail* (1982): 104

---

The house is set on pilings. Its sloping form echoes the dunes that protect it and provides ocean views from as many rooms as possible. The lowest level groups four bunk-bedrooms (sleeping eight) with a screened porch and a bath. On the second level are a sundeck and a large living room open to the view. The central space is interrupted by the master bedroom, which bridges it. High on the third floor, a

prismatic window in the bedroom frames a view over the dunes to the broad beach beyond. A yellow spiral stair joins the wedge to a three-story service block that houses bathrooms, kitchen, and laundry.

Honorable Mention, AIA Middle Atlantic Regional Conference, 1969

*Architecture and Urbanism,* Nov. 1973: 152
*Baltimore Sun Magazine,* Aug. 29, 1971: 28–29
*House Beautiful,* Nov. 1969: 138–141
Mutsch-Engel, A. *Wohnen unter schragem Dach* (1975): 66–67
*Washingtonian,* June 1970: 50–59
*Washington Post,* Oct. 19, 1969: 41

---

See page 48.

Award for Excellence in Apartment Design, *Architectural Record,* 1971
Merit Award, AIA Middle Atlantic Regional Conference, 1971
Award for Excellence in Architecture, Metropolitan Washington Board of Trade, 1971

*Architectural Record,* May 1971
*Architecture and Urbanism,* Oct. 1973: 76–79
*New York Times,* Dec. 26, 1971: 18
*New York Times Magazine,* Jan. 10, 1971: 68–69
*Toshi–Jutaku,* Apr. 1979: 50
*Washington Post,* Sept. 6, 1969; Mar. 6, 1971
*Washington Star,* Nov. 19, 1971; Oct. 11, 1975: E1

---

The illusion of greater space was created here by employing effective lighting in tandem with ceiling and wall mirrors. The bar, tables, and paneling are made of white oak. The original bar stools are actually brass-plated tractor seats.

Award for Excellence for Design of Interiors, *Architectural Record,* 1970
Award for Interior Design, *Institutions and Mass Feeding Magazine,* 1972

*Architectural Record,* Jan. 1970
Davern, J. M. ed. *Places for People* (1976): 144–145
Gordon, B. ed. *Interior Spaces Designed by Architects* (1974): 154–155
*Institutions Volume Feeding,* Dec. 1, 1971

**Eichholz Greenhouse**
Washington, D.C., 1970

## 1971
Fellow of the American Institute of Architects

John Fitzgerald Kennedy Memorial Fellowship awarded by the New Zealand government

Delivered the Kennedy Memorial Fellowship Lectures at Auckland, Otago, Waikato, and Wellington Universities in New Zealand

**Blumenthal House**
Eastern Shore, Maryland, 1971

**House in the Virgin Islands**
Estate Carlton, St. Croix, 1971

**Harvey House**
Northern Virginia, 1971

**Moses House**
McLean, Virginia, 1971

## 1972

**Schwaikert House**
Northwestern Connecticut, 1972

**Renwick Gallery**
Washington, D.C., 1972

326

This semi-detached, early-19th-century row house had the advantage of a large, luxurious south garden. Missing were a greenhouse for the wife and a garage for the husband. So a greenhouse over a garage was added. The new structure's roof, clad in solar-gray glass with standing battens on its east facade, has the appearance of black tin, in keeping with the established materials and domestic scale of the street. The plants within thrive despite the solar tinting. It was drastically altered in 1986.

*Casa Vogue,* Oct. 1974: 156
*House & Garden,* May 1970: 110–111
*House & Garden Remodeling Guide,* Fall 1972–73: 94–95
Melhorn, W. *House & Garden's Book of Remodeling:* 134
National Trust For Historic Preservation *Old and New Architecture Design Relationships* (1980): 111
*New York Times,* Apr. 20, 1970: 40

*Washington Post,* Mar. 14, 1976: E1; Sept. 2, 1979
Weston, M. L. *Decorating with Plants* (1978): 104

See page 52.

Award for Excellence in Architecture, *Architectural Record,* 1971
Honor Award, AIA Middle Atlantic Region, 1971

*Architectural Record,* May 1971
*Architecture and Urbanism,* Nov. 1973: 157
Smith, H. L. Jr., AIA, *25 Years of Record Houses* (1981): 84–87
Wagner, W. F. Jr., FAIA, ed. *Great Houses* (1976): 76
*Washington Post,* May 22, 1971: E8
*Washington Star,* Aug. 20, 1971: D7

See page 60.

First Honor Award, AIA with *American Home* and *House & Home,* Homes for Better Living Program, 1972

*American Home,* Sept. 1972: 58
*Architecture and Urbanism,* Apr. 1974: 93
*Casa Vogue,* July/Aug. 1972: 36–39
*House & Garden,* Dec. 1971: 72–77
Moody, E. *Decorative Art in Modern Interiors* (1977): 46–49
*Washington Post,* July 9, 1972
*Washington Star,* Oct. 1, 1975
Weston, M. L. *Decorating with Plants* (1978): 133

This hillside house on a wooded site was clad in bleached cypress, which quickly weathered gray. The large deck opens every room to a view of the changing colors of the flora.

Award for Excellence in Architecture, Metropolitan Washington Board of Trade, 1971
Merit Award, AIA with *American Home* and *House & Home,* Homes for Better Living Program, 1972
Honor Award, Northern Virginia Chapter/AIA, 1973

*American Home,* Sept. 1972: 54
*House & Home,* Aug. 1972: 80–81
*House Beautiful,* Mar. 1972: 66–71
*Providence Journal,* Aug. 17, 1973
*Washington Post,* July 9, 1972; June 17, 1973
*Washington Star,* Nov. 19, 1971; July 27, 1973

This pavilioned house for a young lawyer and his growing family was designed to take maximum advantage of its wonderful woodland site with a long view to the Potomac Valley. Built of plywood, it was sprayed with a then-patented (and entirely successful) plastic coating whose texture and appearance recalled stucco.

See page 68.

Award for Excellence in Architecture, *Architectural Record,* 1973

*Architectural Record,* May 1973: 54–57
*Architecture and Urbanism,* Nov. 1973: 66
Hoffman, J. *Der offene Kamin* (1977): 40
*House Beautiful,* July 1973: 52–53
*House Beautiful Building Manual,* Spring 1974: cover; Fall 1974–75: 116–121
*House Beautiful's Vacation Homes,* tenth edition (1974): cover

See page 72.

Special Citation for Historic Preservation, Potomac Valley Chapter/AIA, 1972
Award for Excellence in Design, General Services Administration, 1975

*AIA Journal,* Mar. 1972: 8
*Architectural Record,* Jan. 1972; July 1972: 110–111; Aug. 1973: 134–135
*Buildings for the Arts* (1978): 88–90
Craig, L. *The Federal Presence: Architecture, Politics, and Symbols in United States Government Buildings:* 522
Daven, J. M. ed. *Architecture, 1970–1980, A Decade of Change* (1980): 51–52

Diamonstein, B. *Buildings Reborn* (1078): 236
*Georgetowner,* Jan. 27, 1972
Huxtable, A. L. *Goodbye History, Hello Hamburger* (1986): 66, 85, 96
Huxtable, A. L. *Kicked A Building Lately?* (1976): 246–258, 269
*New York Times,* Jan. 28, 1972: 24; May 9, 1976: 31–32; Feb. 17, 1979: 65–70

*Regardie's,* Apr. 1986: 44–57
Thompson, E. K., FAIA, ed. *Recycling Buildings* (1977): 93, 146–148
*Washington Post,* Jan. 22, 1972: B1; Jan. 23, 1972: H1; Jan. 26, 1972: B1; Jan. 13, 1973: E19; Apr. 27, 1974: E1, B1, B5; July 6, 1975
*Washington Post Potomac Magazine,* Feb. 1, 1970: 13; Jan. 30, 1972: 9
*Washington Star,* Jan. 23, 1972: B5; Feb. 20, 1972

**Anatolia College Gymnasium**
Panorama, Greece

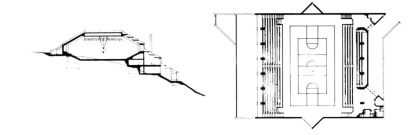

**1973**

**Lincoln Memorial Bookstore**
Parks and History Association
National Park Service
Washington, D.C., 1973

**A House in the Country**
Fort Washington, Pennsylvania, 1973

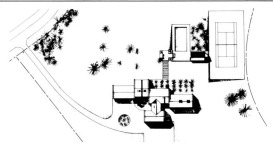

**Half Moon Bay Hotel**
Antigua, West Indies, 1973

**1974**
National Honor Award, American Institute of Architects, the Renwick Gallery: *A masterpiece of creative preservation . . . a lesson which should be applied in every town and city with older buildings that should be kept and used.* — Jury comment

Honorary Degree of Doctor of Humane Letters awarded by Gettysburg College

**S. Korman Apartment**
Philadelphia, Pennsylvania, 1974

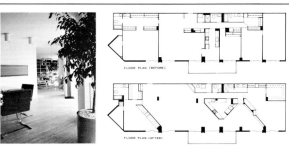

**Peterson Apartment**
Gracie Square, New York City, 1974

**Dumbarton Oaks Library Project**
Washington, D.C., 1974

Financed by the U.S. Department of State's Agency for International Development, this gymnasium serves an American school for Greek children located on a hilltop overlooking Salonika with Mount Olympus in the distance.

Among the neighboring academic structures, the building appears to be a single story tall, while seating 1,500. The natural slope of the grade allowed the inclusion of not only a gymnasium and its supporting facilities, but a much needed art studio and teaching center as well.

*Architectural Record,* "Five Current Projects by Hugh Newell Jacobsen," May 1974: 117

---

*We entered what we can best describe as the inside of a jewel box. The store, as architect Hugh Newell Jacobsen designed it (on a minimal budget), is lined — floor, walls, ceiling and all — in deep blue carpeting, lighted to a pleasantly velvety effect. The small room downstairs features only a counter, an attractive sales girl, a display of color slides that are for sale and a sweeping staircase, also lined in blue carpeting and sporting a dashing chromed railing.*

*The books are on a second level, which Mr. Jacobsen built into the hall, displayed on bright, white shelves and they are all about Abraham Lincoln. —* "Store in the Temple" (editorial), *Washington Post,* Apr. 4, 1973, © The Washington Post.

*Architectural Record,* Aug. 1973: 134–135
Thompson, E. K., FAIA, ed. *Recycling Old Buildings* (1977): 92
*Washington Post,* Apr. 4, 1973
*Washington Star,* June 9, 1974: 14

---

The owner's cogent program called for a large country house sited in an idyllic, broad green meadow, and demanded nearly the same plan as a previously designed house that addressed the sea and reflected the vernacular architecture of its neighbors (see Blumenthal). The same concept of white pavilions also seemed suitable in the middle of a meadow. Not very often can one concept in architecture be built, restudied, and hopefully improved. The dimensions were changed and additional rooms and interior spaces were added without altering the impact of the form upon the land.

First Honor Award, AIA with *American Home* and *House & Home,* Homes for Better Living Program, 1975
Award for Excellence in Architecture, *Architectural Record,* 1975

*Architectural Record,* May 1975: 70–73
Davern, J. *Architecture 1970–1980* (1978): 142
*House & Home,* May 1975: 83
*House Beautiful,* June 1974: 43–50
*House Beautiful Building Manual,* Fall 1975–76: cover, 102–107
*Washington Star,* June 20, 1975: C15

---

This partially realized project is sited on one of the most perfect bays in the Caribbean. The first phase of the work rehabilitating and doubling the size of the existing hotel, refurnishing a new 100-room complex, and designing a complete graphics package, including a logo, staff uniforms, and beachwear — was accomplished. The second phase, never begun, was to have consisted of a village of condominiums sited on a beautiful hill 200 feet above Half Moon Bay.

*Architectural Record,* "Five Current Projects by Hugh Newell Jacobsen," May 1974: 117

---

After all partitions were removed — revealing structural columns, plumbing stacks, ducts, vents, and conduits rising from 10 floors of apartments below — the contraints of this design problem were clearly exposed. The kitchen and baths were located near the plumbing risers. The entry door was relocated. New partitions were placed at a 45-degree angle to the exterior wall (which runs parallel to the public corridor), making the unit appear larger than it actually is. Large skylights were included in the ceilings of the kitchen, bath, and powder rooms.

---

This vintage duplex apartment in a building on Gracie Square overlooking the East River was remodeled principally on the entry level, which includes the living room, dining room, kitchen, library, and foyer. All rooms except the kitchen have truly magnificent views of the river and its ever-changing qualities of light. Our efforts took advantage of this gift by enlarging the windows, removing and relocating walls, "cleaning up" interior details, and designing new lighting and furnishings.

*House Beautiful,* Nov. 1974: 118–121
*House Beautiful Home Remodeling,* Spring 1976: 200–203

---

A 25,000-square-foot library to house an august Byzantine collection was sited underground to preserve the integrity of one of the most beautiful gardens and houses in the United States. The project was never realized.

*Washington Post,* Feb. 16, 1976: D1–D3
*Washington Star,* Mar. 19, 1986: 1, 19

**Schumacher House**
Georgetown, Washington, D.C., 1974

**1975**

**Joseph Baker House**
Frederick, Maryland, 1975
*Project architect: Rodger Speas*

**1976**

**Arts and Industries Building**
Washington, D.C., 1976

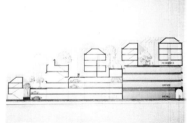

**Pool House Addition**
Bethesda, Maryland, 1976
*Project architect: Frank Riefschneider*

**"Housing on the Avenue"**—
Pennsylvania Avenue Development
Corporation
Washington, D.C., 1976

**Elliott House**
Chevy Chase, Maryland, 1976

**1977**

**Kurtz House**
Washington, D.C., 1977
*Project architect: Rodger Speas*

330

The rear of this small Georgetown townhouse was opened up on two levels, to bring light into those rooms with a southern exposure. The lower-level living/dining room was expanded by removing interior partitions and installing wall-to-wall fixed and sliding glass panels; the room overlooks a new deck with an overhead sunscreen and intimate garden

beyond. The upper level was transformed into a light-filled artist's studio.

---

See page 76.

Award for Excellence in House Design, *Architectural Record,* 1976

*Architectural Record,* May 1976: 82
Heyne, P. *Today's Architectural Mirror* (1982): 31–32
Hoffman, J. *Der offene Kamin* (1977): 105
*House & Garden,* Nov. 1975: 120–123
*House & Garden Building Guide,* Fall 1976: 60–63
Mutsch-Engel and Koch *Wohnen schragen Dach* (1977): 66

*United,* May 1982: 62
Weston, M. L. *Decorating with Plants* (1978): 105

---

See page 82.

First Award for Excellence in Historic Preservation and Architectural Design, AIA Washington Metropolitan Chapter, 1976

*AIA Journal,* The Annual of American Architecture, 1980: 120–123
*AIA Journal,* "Fashion and Fancy on Review," May 1980
Applewhite, E. J. *Washington Itself* (1981): 192
*Architectural Record,* Nov. 1976; May 1980: cover, 42
*Construction News,* May 1980, Honor Awards

Craig, L. *The Federal Presence: Architecture, Politics, and Symbols in United States Government Buildings*
*Interiors,* May 1980: 142–143
Post, R. C. ed. *1876: A Centennial Exhibition* (1976)
Ray, K. *Contextual Architecture, Responding to Existing Style:* 21–26
Schmertz, M. F., FAIA, ed. *New Life for Old Buildings* (1982): 28, 40–45

*Smithsonian,* May 1976: 37
*Walls and Ceilings,* Apr. 1981: 10–11
*Washington Post,* May 9, 1976; May 25, June 14, 1980

---

An indoor swimming pool was attached to the client's semi-Colonial-style brick house. The design deliberately pushed the mass of the wood frame addition into the ground. The roof pitch of the main house was copied and the planes of the roof interrupted to maintain a domestic scale. Inside, dazzling light passes through skylights and transoms and reflects off of the water's

surface. An airlock isolates the atmosphere of the room from that of the main house.

*House & Garden,* Oct. 1976: 104

---

*The designers of the Pennsylvania Avenue Development Corporation, assisted by architect Hugh Newell Jacobsen, have come up with an intriguing idea. To make their "grand axis" a bit more human and lively, they propose to build a neighborly village community of little townhouses east of the forbidding FBI building and across from the Archives. Looking inward, these townhouses crane their necks, as it were, to peer down on*

*an intimate little square. On the outside, however, they are raised above several layers of shops and offices to keep the whole complex in scale with the 10-story offices along the rest of the avenue. The designers show slides of the arcaded Rue de Rivoli in Paris and similar architectural beauties to give you an idea what this facade might look like. — "Town-houses on the Avenue," Washington Post, Dec. 7, 1973, © The Washington Post.*

*Architectural Record,* "Five Current Projects by Hugh Newell Jacobsen," May 1974: 117
*Baumeister,* Dec. 1974: 1314–1317
Gutheim, F. A. *The Federal City: Plans and Realities* (1976): 96–97
*Journal of Housing,* Sept. 1974
*New York Times,* Oct. 10, 1977
*Washington Star,* Apr. 16, 1974
*Washingtonian,* Aug. 1974: 19, 62

---

See page 92.

Award for Excellence in House Design, *Architectural Record,* 1977
Award of Merit, AIA with *American Home* and *House & Home,* Homes for Better Living Program, 1977

Award of Merit for Excellence in Historic Preservation and Architectural Design, Washington Metropolitan Chapter/AIA, 1977

*Architectural Record,* May 1977; May 1978
Brolin, B. C. *Architecture in Context* (1980): 74–75
House & Garden, May 1977: 142–145

*House & Garden Remodeling Guide,* Spring 1978: 94–97
*Preservation News,* Apr. 1978: 1
*Progressive Architecture,* Apr. 1978: 33
Ray, K. *Contextual Architecture, Responding to Existing Style:* 65–66
Schmertz, M. F., FAIA, ed. *New Life for Old Buildings* (1982): 162–163

Smith, H. L. Jr., AIA, *25 Years of Record Houses* (1981): 168–169
*U.S. News & World Report,* July 17, 1978: 67
*Washington Post,* Oct. 22, 1977: C1
*Washington Post Magazine,* Sept. 25, 1977
*Washington Star,* July 30, 1977
*Washington Star Sunday Magazine,* Apr. 9, 1978: 17
Werner, F. *New Living in Old Houses* (1981): 74–77

---

This late-19th-century Georgetown townhouse was virtually rebuilt from the inside out. It received a remodeled and expanded kitchen/breakfast area addition on the garden level, and an enlarged living room with roof terrace on the second level, and new lighting and baths elsewhere.

### Three Linked Pavilions
Washington, D.C., 1977
*Project architect: Rodger Speas*

### A Country House
Virginia, 1977

### Baer House
New York City, 1977

### 1978
National Honor Award, American Institute of Architects, the Elliott House: *Sensitive details originating from the existing house become part of the new design in a solution that is simple and creative. The feeling of openness and space are achieved with a minimum of glass. It is beautifully done.*—Jury comment

### The Design House
Reston, Virginia, 1978
*Project architect: Frank Riefschneider*

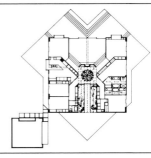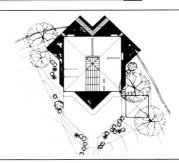

### National Headquarters of the International Union of Bricklayers and Allied Craftsmen
Washington, D.C., 1978
*Project architect: Rodger Speas*

### The Burling Solarium
Georgetown, Washington, D.C., 1978

### Kingdon House
Chevy Chase, Maryland, 1978
*Project architect: Peter Donovan*

A vacant residential lot in Northwest Washington, D.C., with steep grade problems called for a short approach drive off the street to a series of staggered, one-story structures that hug the slope and create a rear deck high in the tree tops. This small two-bedroom residence also includes a spacious artist's studio.

Award of Excellence for House Design, *Architectural Record*, 1978
*Architectural Record*, House of 1978

*Architectural Record*, May 1978
*Nikkei Architecture*, Sept. 4, 1978
*Process Architecture Modern Houses in America* (Japan), 1978: 90
*Washington Home*, Jan. 28, 1988: 16
*Washington Post*, June 22, 1980

---

This project was originally approached as a master plan for several private residences and townhouses on the Virginia shore of the Chesapeake. The client abandoned the idea and built only a single residence for himself and his family.

*House & Garden*, Sept. 1976: 110–113

---

The program called for the remodeling of a 19th-century New York City brownstone. The living room was made two stories tall to take full advantage of views to the redesigned garden.

*House Beautiful*, Jan. 1977: 80–81
*House Beautiful Home Remodeling*, Spring 1978: Cover, 168–169

---

The client, the American Wood Council, called for an exhibit house that would be constructed of as many different wood products as possible. Following this directive, even the foundation walls and footings were successfully specified for wood. Everything else in the program reflects the tenant's requirements and the lakefront site.

Design for Better Living Award, the American Wood Council, 1978

*AE Concepts in Wood Design*, Jan./Feb. 1979: 10–14
*Building Magazine*, Dec. 4, 1978: 74–78
*Casa Vogue*, Mar. 1979: 124
Heyne, P. *Today's Architectural Mirror* (1982): 62–64
*House & Garden*, Oct. 1978: 160–165; Nov. 1978; May 1980: 96–99
*Washington Post*, July 24, 1978: G3, H11

*Washington Star Sunday Magazine*, July 23, 1978: 4–5, 28

---

The project called for the remodeling of office space in a downtown building owned by the client. As the client's needs have expanded, additional space in this building as well as satellite offices in other areas of the country have been designed to reflect the materials and crafts of the union's members.

*Interiors*, June 1979: 116

---

When first purchased by the client in the 1930s, this row house was actually three humble, 19th-century houses. They were already fused and altogether admirably altered to form a single dwelling of comfort and distinction by the time this addition was designed.

*Home Life Magazine*, Sept. 26, 1976 32–33
*House & Garden*, June 1973: 42–43
*House & Garden Remodeling Guide*, Fall 1974: 96–97
*Washington Post*, Mar. 24, 1974: H1, H3; Sept. 2, 1979
Weston, M. L. *Decorating with Plants* (1978): 98

---

Renovation of this Colonial Revival house focused on the creation of informal living spaces that would supply additional light and garden vistas, and the improvement of circulation for indoor-outdoor entertaining. A garden room was added, the garage was converted to a library, and the kitchen was updated. Changes were deliberately kept inconspicuous so that the house—a "house of the year" in 1932—appeared practically unaltered.

Citation for Historic Preservation and Architectural Design, Washington Chapter/AIA, 1980

*Home-Life*, Mar. 18, 1979: cover, 8
*House & Garden*, Nov. 1980: 134–137

**1979**

**Putterman House**
Central Pennsylvania, 1979
*Project architect: Rodger Speas*

**1980**
National Honor Award, American Institute of Architects, the Arts and Industries Building: *Recaptured the essence of the original building without imitation of the past.*—Jury comment

**House in Kentucky**
Lexington, Kentucky, 1980
*Project architect: Rodger Speas*

**A Projected Mausoleum**
Mediterranean Sea, 1980
*Project architect: Stephen Evanusa*

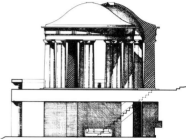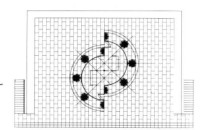

**Challinor House**
Connecticut, 1980
*Project architect: Charles Parker*

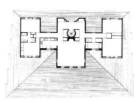

**Deree College Gymnasium and Library, American College of Greece**
Athens, Greece, 1980

**Dixon House**
Long Lake, Minnesota, 1980
*Project architect: Charles Parker*

**Eichholz Apartment**
1980
*Project architect: Rodger Speas*

334

See page 116.

Award for Excellence in House Design, *Architectural Record,* 1980 and 1981

*American Artist,* Feb. 1981: 44–49
*Architectural Record,* Nov. 1978: 113–120;
May 1980: 68–71
*GA Houses,* No. 17, Feb. 1985: 68–93
*House Beautiful,* May 1981: 132–135
*Nikkei Architecture,* 1980: 64–67
*Process: Architecture Modern Wooden Houses,*
1980: 50–55
*Tonconogy Arquitectos,* Apr. 1986

---

See page 136.

First Honor Award, AIA with *Housing,* Homes for Better Living Program, 1981

*Architectural Digest,* Feb. 1981: 120–127, 148
*Architectural Record,* Nov. 1978: 113–120;
June 1981: 44
*Das Haus,* Nov. 1981: 8–13
Heyne, P. *Today's Architectural Mirror*
(1982): 62
Niles, B. *White by Design* (1984): 128–131
*United,* May 1982: 58–63, 103–107

---

The program for this unbuilt mausoleum
called for two places of interment and a
small apartment for visitors. Under the
split 5th-century dome of the brushed
stainless steel pavilion will sit a classic
bronze urn.

*Architectural Record,* "The Gentle Art of
Abstraction," Sept. 1982: 112–119

---

See page 112.

*Architectural Record,* Nov. 1978: 113–120
*New York Times,* Sept. 28, 1980: 26–27
*Portfolio,* 6 (Spring 1982)

---

See page 98.

*Architectural Record,* "Five Current
Projects by Hugh Newell Jacobsen," May
1974: 117–122; Nov. 1985: 194–209

---

See page 104.

Award for Excellence in House Design, *Architectural Record,* 1979
First Honor Award, AIA with *House & Home,* Homes for Better Living Program, 1979

*AIA Journal,* July 1979: 25
*Architectural Record,* Nov. 28, 1978: 113–120;
May 1979: 68–71
*Housing,* Sept. 1979
*Process: Architecture Modern Wooden Houses,*
1980: 44
*Washington Post,* "Barns for Better Living,"
May 26, 1979: E1, E11

---

This 1920s apartment was completely
redesigned to house the owner's sizable
collection of 20th-century art. The
apartment was subdivided into two units,
the smaller sold after the renovation was
completed, the larger retained by the client.

*New York Times,* May 12, 1987: B37

### Dr. Robinson and Jean Baker House
McDonogh, Maryland, 1980, 1988
*Project architects: David Takesue (1980),*
*Ernest Schichler (1988)*

Tau Sigma Delta Silver Medal of
Distinction in Design from Clemson
University

### Mary Livingston Ripley Garden
Washington, D.C., 1981
*Project architect: Paul Roddick*

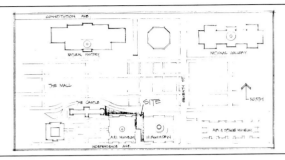

### "Ole Jim"
Washington, D.C., 1981
*Project architect: Paul Roddick*

### The Library for the American University in Cairo
Cairo, Egypt, 1981

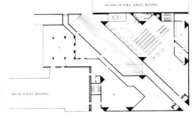

**1982**

### A Desert Guest House
Tucson, Arizona, 1982
*Project architect: Rodger Speas*

### Athens College Theater
District of Psychio, Athens, Greece, 1982
*Accoustical engineer: Alfred Kraas*
*Structural engineer: Robert Hansen*

### Huge House
McLean, Virginia, 1982
*Project architect: Rodger Speas*

The podium created for this distinguished Colonial Revival house permitted the ground-floor windows to be just that; they now allow the floor to meet the ground. A two-story solarium extended the living spaces and expanded the interior both dimensionally and visually toward the newly achieved light.

337

This Victorian garden occupies a sliver of land between the Hirshhorn Museum and the Arts and Industries Building. Conceived as a garden for the handicapped, it serves as an outdoor connection between the Mall and Independence Avenue. Formerly named the East Garden, it was rededicated as the Mary Livingston Ripley Garden in 1988.

This renovation brought new use to a building originally designed as a gymnasium at the nation's first college for the deaf. The building exterior was restored to its original appearance and palette of Victorian colors.

*Washington Post,* June 17, 1979: E2

See page 166.

*Architectural Record,* "Five Current Projects by Hugh Newell Jacobsen," May 1974: 117–122
*Cairo Today,* Apr. 1982: 55
*Town & Country,* Jan. 1985: 104

This project in the desert foothills involved the remodeling of an existing Southwest adobe residence built in the 1930s. The new and relatively small guest house, which contains two bedrooms, a living room, and a kitchen, serves the swimming pool and the main house. The client wanted a retreat from the demands of life at his main residence in the Midwest. Although completely designed, the project for the main house is awaiting construction.

See page 172.

*Architectural Record,* Nov. 1985: 194–209

See page 176.

Award for Distinctive Residential Architecture, *Washingtonian* and the Washington Chapter/AIA

*Architectural Digest,* Sept. 1983: 150–159, 198; Oct. 1984: 84–91
*Washingtonian,* May 1984: 263

**University of Michigan
Alumni Center**
Ann Arbor, Michigan, 1982
*Project architect: Charles Parker*

**Buckwalter House**
Eastern Pennsylvania, 1982
*Project architect: Rodger Speas*

**Fort McNair Unbuilt Project**
Washington, D.C., 1982

**Gettysburg College Library**
Gettysburg, Pennsylvania, 1982
*Project architect: Charles Parker*

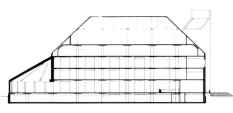

**House on the Eastern Shore**
Maryland, 1982
*Project architect: Charles Parker*

1983

**Zamoiski House**
Eastern Shore, Maryland, 1983
*Project architect: Rodger Speas*

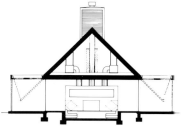

**Saudi Arabia Project**
Northwest Washington, D.C., 1983
*Project architect: Emily Volz*

338

*On a midnight (literally) tour of Ann Arbor I saw your new building which is the only recent building there that looks as though the architect had actually visited the site before starting the design.*—Robert A. M. Stern, letter, April 21, 1982

See page 184.

Award for Achievement of Excellence in Architecture, Washington Chapter/ AIA, 1983
Honor Award for Excellence in Design, AIA Middle Atlantic Region, 1983

*AIA Journal,* Nov. 1983: 61; Nov. 1984: 72–75
*Ann Arbor News,* Oct. 28, 1982: G6; Feb. 20, 1983: G5
*Ann Arbor Observer,* Jan. 1979
*Architectural Quarterly,* June 1985: 72–75
*Architectural Record,* Apr. 1983: 130–137
*Detroit News,* Apr. 2, 1985: D1–D3
*WBC Bulletin,* Jan. 1984: 9

---

*For those who like to eat cake and have it at the same time, that has to be the solution. . . .Both traditionalists and "past traditionalists" can claim victory. And it looks good.*—Hugh Hardy, FAIA

See page 124.

Award for Excellence in House Design, *Architectural Record,* 1981
First Honor Award, AIA with *Housing,* Homes for Better Living Program, 1981

*Architectural Record,* May 1981: 116–121; June 1981: cover, 44
*Casa Vogue,* Oct. 1981: 222–225
Conran, T. *Terrence Conran's New House Book* (1985): cover, 42–43
Donovan, C. *Living Well: The New York Times Book of Home Design and Decoration* (1981): 172–175
*GA Houses,* No. 17, Feb. 1985: 68–93
*Hauser,* Jan. 1984: 10–19, 90–91

*House & Garden,* June 1981: 106–113
*Housing,* May 1981: 44
*New York Times Magazine,* May 3, 1981
*Nikkei Architeeture,* Sept. 14, 1981: 109–112
Niles, B. *White by Design* (1984): 126–127
*Photography,* Mar. 1982
*Toshi Jutaku,* Feb. 1982: 28–31
*Washington Post,* July 26, 1981: B6

---

The National Defense University's campus derives from a 1903 master plan by McKim, Mead and White for the Army War College and Army Engineer School. This architect was commissioned to design new, enlarged and/or reorganized space for the library, administration, National War College, and athletic facilities. Four academic buildings were designed to accommodate the separate departments of the college. The

site is in accord with the master plan, as are the buildings continuing the row of generals' quarters on the western side of the rectangular green, as begun by Stanford White.

*Architectural Record,* "The Gentle Art of Abstraction," Sept. 1982: 112–119

---

See page 152.

Grand Design Award, 1986, and Excellence in Masonry Design Award: Category Institutional, 1986, both awarded by the Masonry Contractors Association of Central Pennsylvania

*AIA Journal,* May 1982: 176–182; Oct. 1982: 77
*Architectural Record,* Sept. 1976
*Brick in Architecture,* 42(3)

---

See page 156.

Award for Excellence in House Design, *Architectural Record,* 1982
First Honor Award, AIA with *Housing,* Homes for Better Living Program, 1982

*Architectural Record,* Nov. 1978: 113–120; May 1982: 58–63
*Hauser,* Jan. 1986: 2, 12–19, 96–97
*House Beautiful,* Feb. 1982: 58–63
*House Beautiful Building Manual,* Winter 1982: 32–37
*Housing,* May 1982: 53; Aug. 1982: 52–53
Kemp, J. *American Vernacular Regional Influences in Architecture and Interior Design* (1987): 140–142

*Nikkei Architecture,* Aug. 30, 1982; 37–40
*Toshi Jutaku,* Feb. 1983: 48–51

---

*The glass skin and stone terrace and floors unite the house with the landscape in a subtle, yet striking harmony. . . . Louvered shutters, which act as sunscreens when raised, cleverly double as protection from the elements and intruders when the house is unoccupied. Expertly and with supreme confidence, the architect has designed a house that displays admirable modesty, skillful composition and detailing, and perfect compatibility with*

*climate and site.*—Jury comment, 1985 AIA Honor Awards Program.

See page 190.

Award for Excellence in House Design, *Architectural Record,* 1984
Honor Award, American Wood Council, 1985

*AIA Journal,* May 1985: 268–273; Mar. 1986: 20
*Architectural Record,* Mid-Apr. 1984: 74–81
*Architecture,* May 1985: 268–273
*Architecture Quarterly,* Fall 1985: cover, 24–29
*Baltimore Sun Magazine,* May 5, 1985: H1
Blumenthal, A. R. ed. *350 Years of Art and Architecture* (1984): 238
*GA Houses,* No. 17, Feb. 1985: 68–93

*House & Garden,* July 1984: 78–85
*House & Garden Decorating Guide,* Summer 1977: 92
*Washington Post,* Apr. 30, 1985: C8; May 16, 1985: 28
*Washington Post Magazine,* May 4, 1986: 14–17, 61–62

---

This complex, in keeping with the domestic scale of its surroundings, was to house the ambassador's family and staff and also serves as a residence for visiting royalty. Ceremonial and informal requirements are integrated and defined at the main entrance.

**Alumni Square**
Georgetown University
Washington, D.C., 1983
*Project architect: Charles Parker*

**Hotel Talleyrand**
Paris, France, 1984
*Project architect: Paul Roddick*

**Karpidas House**
Athens, Greece, 1984
*Project architect: Paul Roddick*

**Welles House**
Bowling Green, Ohio, 1984
*Project architect: Rodger Speas*

**American Embassy Guard House**
Paris, France, 1984
*Project architect: Paul Roddick*

**St. Peter's Church**
Olney, Maryland, 1984
*Project architect: Emily Volz*
*(First design)*

**Spaso House**
Moscow, USSR, 1984
*Project architect: Paul Roddick*

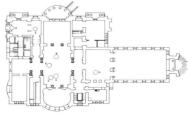

See page 200.

*Architectural Record,* Sept. 1982: 112–119;
Oct. 1984: 148–153
*Regardie's,* Apr. 1986: 44–57
*Washington Post,* Jan. 7, 1987: D1, D6; Jan.
12, 1984: D1, D3

*In the words of Evan G. Galbraith, former
American ambassador to France, "The
restoration of the Hotel Talleyrand is the most
important architectural preservation effort
ever undertaken by the United States overseas."
Thus, thanks to the tenacity of the State
Department and the skill of the architect, the
house has come alive again.*
— Susan Mary Alsop, courtesy of

*Architectural Digest,* Nov. 1984: 190–198
*Connoisseur,* Nov. 1984: 38; Jan. 1987
*Le Figaro,* Sept. 11, 1984
*Preservation News,* June 1985: 13
*State,* June 1981: 28
*USIA World,* Feb. 1985: 6–7

See page 206.

*Architectural Digest,* "Classical Illusions,"
July 1987: 72–77
*Architectural Record,* "The Gentle Art of
Abstraction," Sept. 1982: 112–119

See page 212.

*Architecture,* The 9th Annual Review of
New American Architecture, May 1986:
162–167
*Architektur und Wohnen,* Mar. 1987: 18–26
*House & Garden,* June 1985: 148–157,
194, 196

In response to heightened security
concerns of the Department of State,
American embassies worldwide have been
"hardened." The embassy in Paris, located
on the Place de la Concorde, required a
guard house that would not only be secure
but also fit into its historic context.

A church has been referred to as a house of
families. Here a house of families was
designed to serve as a family of houses. The
church roof repeats the vernacular forms of
the surrounding residential community, its
gables rising successively and extending
the reach of the hill. Four open porches on
the axis points of the cruciform plan
accentuate the pattern created by the tall
arched windows surrounding the building.

Inside, circular windows in each gable
provide clerestory lighting and an
everchanging pattern of natural
illumination that would have been diffused
by white ceilings and walls, and controlled
by interior shutters (see St. Peter's,
page 346).

The residence of the United States'
ambassador in Moscow is located on
Spasopeskovskaya Square in central
Moscow. Its name, Spaso House, is derived
from the square, which in turn is named
after the small Russian Orthodox church
located there, the Church of the Salvation
on the Sands. The house, built in 1914 for a
wealthy merchant and manufacturer, was
designed by Adamovich and Mayat.

Nineteenth-century Russian Neoclassic in
style, it is at once awkwardly heroic and
elegantly irrational.

*Architectural Digest,* Jan. 1988: cover,
130–133, 164
*Washington Post Magazine,* May 26, 1985:
12–15

**1985**

National Honor Award, American Institute of Architects, the Zamoiski House: *A house that displays admirable modesty, skillful composition and detailing, and perfect compatibility with climate and site.*—Jury comment

**Elliott Gazebo**
Chevy Chase, Maryland, 1985
*Project architect: Rodger Speas*

**Rosenak House**
Tesuque, New Mexico, 1985
*Project architect: Rodger Speas*

**Kahn House**
Lima, Ohio, 1985
*Project architect: David Takesue*

**Bricklayers Union International Masonry Institute (Brice House)**
Annapolis, Maryland, 1985
*Project architect: Charles Parker*

**1986**

**AEGIS Corporate Headquarters Project**
Reston, Virginia, 1986
*Project architect: Charles Parker*

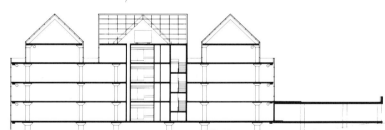

**Faberge Gallery**
Richmond, Virginia, 1986
*Project architect: Paul Roddick*

**St. John's Abbey**
Collegeville, Maryland, 1986
*Project architect: Paul Roddick with Rafferty, Rafferty & Mikutowski Architects*
*Landscape architect: Dan Kiley*

342

The 1986 Wood Remodeling Award, *American Wood Council 1986 Remodeling Awards:* 57

*Architectural Digest,* Apr. 1988: 33
*Architectural Record,* Apr. 1987
*Regardie's,* Apr. 1986: 44–57
*Remodeling,* "Winners of the 1986 Wood Remodeling Design Awards," Feb./Mar. 1987: 62

---

See page 238.

*Global Architecture Houses,* Dec. 22, 1987: 106–111
*House & Garden,* Apr. 1986: 162–169, 233

---

See page 248.

Award for Excellence in House Design, *Architectural Record,* 1986

*Architectural Digest,* "Houses That Work," Nov. 1982
*Architectural Record,* Apr. 1986: 128–133
*Ball State Daily News,* Feb. 8, 1984
*Builder Magazine,* Nov. 1986: 94–97
Harvard University Graduate School of Design catalog, Summer 1987: 4
*House Beautiful,* Sept. 1986: 76–81
*House Beautiful Building Manual,* Summer 1987: 64–69

Kemp, J. *American Vernacular Regional Influences in Architecture and Interior Design* (1987): 106–109
*Regardie's,* Apr. 1986: 44–57
*Schoner Wohnen,* Feb. 1987: 6–12
*Washington Post,* Dec. 10, 1987: 11

---

This 200-year-old landmark American masonry structure is gradually being remodeled and restored with faithful attention to its original details by its new owner, the International Union of Bricklayers and Allied Craftsmen. The programmed functions include meeting facilities, a library, and a museum dedicated to the history of masonry techniques, materials, and craftsmanship.

---

To overcome the limitations of the site, the design for this unbuilt corporate headquarters calls for a building of six interconnected pavilions located directly over the lake. The reinforced concrete structure distributes 48,000 square feet of space over its four stories. All facades feature flush reflective insulating glass (attached to interior mullions by a butt-glazed silicon joint system) that offers floor-to-ceiling views from the interior. The reflective glass roof, pitched at 45 degrees is an extension of the vertical glass-wall system. Nearly every office has a view of the lake and other pavilions, and a reflection of both.

---

Designed to display more than 200 objects, including five Imperial Eggs designed by the famous jeweler to the czar, this permanent exhibit is housed in a 1930s building also renovated by the architect.

*Richmond News Leader,* "Let There Be Light," June 4, 1985

---

This master plan responded to the current and projected needs of Saint John's Abbey, a Benedictine community comprised of an all-male undergraduate college, a coed graduate school of theology, and a coed preparatory high school, as well as the abbey itself.

**Voorhees House**
Nantucket, Massachusetts, 1987
*Project architect: Rodger Speas*

**Mendoza House**
Dominican Republic, 1987
*Project architects: John Murphey,
Ernest Schichler*

**Bryan House**
Worthington Valley, Maryland, 1987
*Project architects: S.E., Paul Roddick*
*Landscape architect: Dan Kiley*

**House on the Gulf**
Florida 1987
*Project architect: Paul Roddick*

**Palmedo House**
Long Island, New York, 1987
*Project architect: Charles Parker*

**1988**
National Honor Award, American Institute
of Architects, the Mendoza House: *Great care
has been taken with extraordinary details, from
the swimming pool, which seems to fuse with
the horizon, to the locally inspired architect-
designed furnishings and weather vane, to the
sun-controlling breezeways, courtyards,
louvers, and high ceilings.* — Jury comment

Elected associate to the National Academy
of Design

**Advaney House**
The Netherlands, 1988
*Project architect: Rodger Speas*

**Jacobs House**
Meadowbrook, Pennsylvania, 1988
*Project architect: Paul Roddick*

See page 264.

*House & Garden,* Aug. 1987: 78–81

This house looks toward the sea through a coconut grove. In front, sand serves as lawn and lawn as drive. The composition is given order by the rows of more than 100 palm trees. Each of the house's seven pavilions is trimmed in a sun-bleached pastel. See page 278.

*House & Garden,* Dec. 1987: 118
*House & Garden,* May 1988: Cover (Bohio)
*Architecture,* May 1988: 192

This large stone residence has been designed to appear as an informal gathering of farm buildings in rural Maryland's horse country. See page 268.

*Architectural Digest,* July 1988

This southern Florida house, sited 50 yards from the Gulf of Mexico, takes advantage of its wonderful views. Set high on a podium, the house opens to the water, yet maintains the owner's privacy from the beach.

This house is sited in a broad and open meadow between a large, old oak and a reaching expanse of open cove that leads to Long Island Sound. The oak and the architecture combine to hide the water until it is framed by the house, which turns the strong, central axis formed by the entrance drive and the chimney mass 45 degrees toward the cove and the view.

Designed in six parts, with its entry and stair enclosed separately, the house is composed of successive pavilions that are tightly aligned in symmetrical pairs at their gable ends. The pavilion facades match one another as they reduce in size and maintain a balance on either side of the chimney mass. Each pavilion houses an individual function, and three of the pavilions contain second-floor spaces.

The design of the house is disciplined by an implied order based on a single square, with multiples forming larger squares, double squares, and so on, and with the rooflines following the diagonals of the squares. The house was completed and occupied in 1988.

See page 288.

*ASAP Magazine,* Mar. 1988 (American Society of Architectural Perspectivists)

**Forbes House**
Bloomfield Hills, 1988
*Project architect: Rodger Speas*

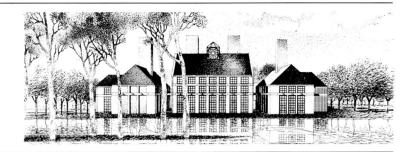

**Carson House**
Dutchess County, New York, 1988
*Project architect: John Murphey*

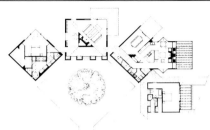

**St. Peter's II**
Olney, Maryland, 1988
*Project architect: Paul Roddick*
*Liturgical consultant: Frank Kacmarcik*

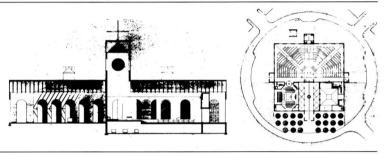

**A Greek Villa**
Greece, 1988
*Project architect: Paul Roddick*

**Hillside House in Greece**
Athens, Greece, 1978
*Project architect: Paul Roddick*
*Structural engineer: Basil Kolias*

**Waddell House**
Long Island, New York, 1988
*Project architect: Jamshid Kooros*

**Hillside House Overlooking
the River**
McLean, Virginia, 1978
Addition 1988
*Project architects: Rodger Speas (1978
original house), Ernest Schichler (1988
addition)*

See page 296.

See page 300.

Following the congregation's request for a more "Colonial" building, this cruciform, white brick structure contains a series of arched windows. In plan, the project contains a main worship area for 800 participants, a daily chapel seating 250, a fellowship hall for a convivial 300, and a central commons holding 300, all following the guidelines of Vatican II and the American Council of Bishops.

High on the side of an abandoned rock quarry are two villas, built by business partners who wanted to take advantage of the remarkable views over the ancient and historic plain of Attica below.

The site falls rapidly away from the street. This resulting multilevel villa is an abstraction of the Greek hilltown. White cubes arranged with terraces and pergolas help the scheme come to terms with site and zoning. The dome, which actually houses a staircase, completes the evocation of a village as it rises against the ever-blue sky of Greece. The house is scheduled to be completed in 1988.

*Architectural Record,* "The Gentle Art of Abstraction," Sept. 1982: 112–119

Designed in a vernacular palette of colors and materials—white concrete walls and dark green marble floors—this house steps down the mountainside, its series of terraces and sunscreens are deliberately abstracted from the Palace of Knossos on Crete. There, the column was painted red; here, the similarly proportioned columns are clad in mirror-finished chrome that should dazzle in the Grecian light. A shared tennis court was fitted between the two villas of its owners, embedded 22 feet into the rock at one end and extending 20 feet out of the rock at the other; the flights of errant balls were not considered. Like its neighbor, this villa is expected to be completed in 1988.

*Architectural Record,* Sept. 1982: 112–119
*New York Times,* Dec. 8, 1985: B8

See page 304.

This hard-edged nearly classical Modern house consists of two two-story cubes that are rotated 45 degrees away from the parallel (as determined by the steep slope) and whose lower, rectangular massing (housing service spaces for the larger cubes) adheres conventionally to the grade. The living and dining rooms occupy the upper levels, taking advantage of wonderful and changing views of the turbulent Potomac River far below.

*Architectural Digest,* "Houses That Work," Nov. 1982

**1964**
Washington Post, *Nov. 10*
*(Isham House)*

**1966**
Washington Post Potomac Magazine,
*Nov. 20 (Sohier House)*

**1967**
Washington Star, *Jan. 25: G4*
*(Corcoran Gallery)*

**1969**
Baltimore Magazine, *June 15*
*(Washington Theater Club)*
House Beautiful Home Remodeling,
*Spring/Summer (Jewett and Cord
Meyer Houses)*
Look, *Sept. 23 (Porter House)*

**1970**
Georgetowner, *May 7 (HNJ)*
Washington Post Magazine, *"Potomac
People," July 26*

**1971**
Architectural Record, *Jan.: 94–95 (King
of the Road Motor Inn)*
Georgetowner, *Sept. 12 (New Zealand)*
New England Listener, *Nov. 1–7: 15
(reprint of interview broadcast in
New Zealand, Oct. 3)*
Washington Post, *Jan. 2 (Embassy
Row); "New Town, Old Woes," Feb. 14:
K1–5; Mar. 21: G1 (city facades, real
buildings); Apr. 5 (reply); "That Do It
All," Aug. 8*
Washington Star, *Jan. 7 (Children's
Hospital)*
Washingtonian, *Sept.*

**1972**
Richmond News Leader, *"Good
Architecture Is Defined," Sept. 13*
Virginia Museum Bulletin, *"Virginia
Architects/Planners 1972": 11*

**1973**
Washington Post, *May 6: L1
(Wolf House)*

**1974**
Grand Rapids Press, *Sept. 1 (HNJ)*
Washington Post Potomac Magazine,
*Mar. 3: 36*

**1975**
*Hawkins, A.* The Architectural
Cookbook, *"Stew Newell Jacobsen": 27*
Interiors, *"Interior Awards Verdict
from the Jury," Jan.: 156*

**1976**
*Bundesen, L.* U.S. People of Washington,
D.C.: *98–99*
House & Garden, *May: 114–115 (King
House); Aug.: 79 (the "Strip")*
*Wrenn, T. and Mulloy, E.* America's
Forgotten Architecture

**1977**
Home Life Magazine, *May 22: 14,
(Cleveland Park, redwood deck);
Oct. 30: 13 (HNJ library); Nov. 13: 10
(solar energy)*
House & Garden, *June: 108–109 (Field
House); Dec. (HNJ Christmas tree)*
Washingtonian, *"Good Thinking,"
Sept.: 109*

**1978**
Buildings for the Arts, *the editors of
Architectural Record*
*Diamonstein, B.* Buildings Reborn:
*236–237*
House & Garden Remodeling Guide,
*Spring/Summer: cover, 110–111 (Feild
House)*
New York Times, *May 7: 1 (house
stoops)*
*Von Eckardt, W.* Back to the Drawing
Board! Planning Livable Cities
Washington Post, *Jan. 8: L2 (Rust
House)*
Washington Post, *"The Architect Who
Understands Social and Visual
Dynamics," May 14: F1 (I. M. Pei)*

**1979**
AIA Journal, *May: 70–71 (sand castle)*
AIA Memo, *Apr. 16 (sand castle)*
Burlington Vermont Free Press, *"Super
Sandcastle," Apr. 8*
Charleston News Courier, *Jan. 21
(architects to review hotel design)*
*Drexler, A.* Transformations in Modern
Architecture
Home Life Magazine, *Feb. 25 (home
improvements); Mar. 18: 8 (skylights);
May 20: cover, 8–13 (sand castle)*
Interiors, *Apr.: 80 (chairperson, AIA
awards)*
*Johnson, P.* Philip Johnson,
Writings: *206*
Kansas City *(Kansas City/AIA): 160
(Kemper House)*
New York Times, *"A Castle 'Just for
Fun,'" Apr. 4*
Philadelphia Inquirer, *"Just for Fun,"
Apr. 4 (AIA exhibit, sand castle)*
Savannah Gazette, *Jan. 15: 7 (lecture)*
Savannah Morning News, *Apr. 25
(lecture)*
Smithsonian Associate, *Buildings
Reborn (symposium), Mar. 1, 5;
Architectural Update: Buildings Reborn
(class), Mar. 12; Architects at Home
(tour), May 1*
Washington Post, *"Fathoming the
Depths of the Great Thaw of 1979"
Mar. 4: G1; Apr. 3: B7 (sand castle);
"Building on a Human Scale,"
Apr. 22: N1*
Wisconsin Architect, *Apr.: 21*

**1980**
Home-Life, *Apr. 20: 13 (Rust Pool)*
Progressive Architecture, *"International
Interiors," Sept.: 167*

**1981**
Historic Preservation, *Sept./Oct.: 21
(preservation of old buildings)*

**1982**
*Heyne, P.* Today's Architectural Mirror
Mobile, Alabama Azalea City News &
Review, *"New Architecture for Old
Districts," Apr. 29: 14–15*
People, *July 13: 118–119 (Onassis
House)*
Washington Dossier, *"Georgetown
Neighbors," July: cover, 14*
Washington Post, *June 13, 1982*
Washington Times, *"Diana Hears,"
Oct. 28: B1*

**1983**
Sunset, *Apr.: 280; Oct.: 100 (Western
Home Awards Jury)*

**1984**
Architectural Digest, *"Architect's Travel
Notes Hugh Newell Jacobsen in Cairo,"
Feb.: 204*
Architectural Record, *"The telling
detail, I: Houses by Hugh Newell
Jacobsen," Feb.: 138; "The telling detail,
II: Institutional buildings," Mar.: 152;
"Roundtable: Architectural Education,"
June: 51*
Grand Rapids Press, *Sept. 1 (HNJ)*
Interiors, *July: 39 (awards jury)*
New York Times, *"Two Washingtonians
with a Capital W," May 3: B8*
Washington Post, *"New Order: Date
Books of the Rich and Famous—and
Just Folks, Too" Dec. 31: D1*

**1985**
AIA Memo, *Jan. 23: 3*
Arcade *(Seattle Chapter/AIA), May
(lecture)*
Architectural Digest, *"Architect's Travel
Notes Hugh Newell Jacobsen in
Antwerp—Harbor of Tradition and
Order," Mar.: 86; May: 210 (Stern
House)*
Arizona Republic, *Oct. 6: 82 (Arizona
AIA Design Conference)*
Broadsheet *(Baltimore Chapter/AIA),
Jan./Feb. (excerpts from* Architectural
Digest*)*
Construction News, *July 26: 24 (AIA
convention panel)*
*Diamonstein, B.* American Architecture
Now II: *134–144*
Fairfax Journal, *Aug.: A1 (Pleasant
Grove Methodist Church)*
Interiors, *Jan.: 156; Mar.: 42 (AIA
convention)*
Metropolitan Home, *June: 67 (Rust
Pool)*
Magazine of Sigma Chi, *"There are no
laws . . . just what works," Winter: 15*
San Francisco Examiner, *"Architects
Tour City's Backwoods," Aug. 14: A1*
Vero Beach Press-Journal, *July 21: 6E
(Schaub House)*

Washington Dossier, *"Washington's
Mighty 500," Jan.: 84*
Washington Post, *"Travails Around the
World," Aug. 22: B2; "Gerald Hines and
the Well-Built Empire," Aug. 27: C2*
Washington Times, *"The Beauty of
Brick," Feb. 28: 5M; "Washington
Architect with Designs on the World,"
June 6: M1*

**1986**
Regardies, *"House Calls," Apr.: 41–57*
Seattle Times, *"Homes of the Year," Feb.
23: E1 (Seattle AIA Jury); "Architect
Picks Winning House," Feb. 27: C2*

**1987**
Architectural Digest, *"Architects
Review Lighting," Sept.: 12*
House Beautiful, *Dec.: 32 (home design)*

**1988**
Washington Post, Washington Home,
*"Exploring Personalities in
Architecture," Feb. 4: 26*
Smithsonian Associate, *"A Decade of
D.C. Architecture," Feb./Mar.*

# Credits

All photographs are by Robert C. Lautman, and all renderings are by Stephen S. Evanusa, except as follows:

Jaime Ardiles-Arce, reproduced with permission from *Architectural Digest* 228–231, 232 *top right, bottom right,* 233–235, 340 (Hotel Talleyrand)
Ralph Bogertman 114–115
R. Frasier 316
Marianne Haas, reproduced with permission from *Architectural Digest* 208–211, 344
Mick Hales 254, 260
John M. Hall 265–267
Balthazar Korab Ltd. 153–155, 338 (Gettysburg *left*)
Latour Rossel Communications Inc. 50 *middle*
Norman McGrath 33–35, 49, 50 top, 51, 318 (Carter), 320 (Shaw), 322 (Jacobsen, Millet), 324 (Tidesfall), 328 (Peterson), 332 (Baer)
United States Embassy in France 340 (American Embassy Guard House)
Bent Rej 158–165, 338 (House on the Eastern Shore)
Jim Weaver 345 (House on the Gulf), 352

The following photographs by Lautman are reproduced with permission from:
*Architectural Digest* 65–67, 140–141, 143, 147, 149–151, 177–179, 181–183
*House Beautiful,* Copyright © September 1986, The Hearst Corporation, All rights reserved. 250–263
*House & Garden* 61, 63, 78–79, 93, 94, 128–132, 134, 192, 194–196, 214–215, 218, 220–223, 225, 239–241, 242 top right, 243–244, 245 top right, bottom left, bottom right, 324 (Smernoff), 342 (Buckwalter, Zamoiski)

Illustrations, page 8: Copyright 1977 Louis I. Kahn Collection, University of Pennsylvania and Pennsylvania Historical and Museum Commission

The photographs that
illuminate these pages are
largely the work of Robert C.
Lautman. I like to think that
the growth of our friendship
has paralleled the growth of
the mutal understanding of
our respective disciplines.
Bob not only knows
(exquisitely) just where to
stand at *the* particular
moment, but also how sharply
to focus his unique,
incredible eye.—H.N.J.